Mallarmé

INSOLUBILIA: NEW WORK IN CONTEMPORARY PHILOSOPHY

Series Editors: A.J. Bartlett, Justin Clemens and Jon Roffe

Insolubilia are problems that one cannot solve, cannot salve and cannot save—but which nonetheless cannot be avoided. This series publishes works that engage with the problems that deserve the name contemporary because they arise in and pertain specifically to our contemporary situation. These necessarily novel works will explore foundational questions in philosophy from a new perspective, offer new syntheses of previously disparate fields of investigation with an eye to the contemporary problematic, and think through in a rigorous way the relationship between previously heterogeneous concerns that have now come into contact (e.g. critical theory and the environment; philosophy and the market; neuroscience and poetry). Insolubilia is accordingly a series that publishes the latest works in continental philosophy that incarnate, present, and engage the insolubles of our time.

Titles in the Series:

Mallarmé: Rancière, Milner, Badiou by Robert Boncardo and Christian R. Gelder

Mallarmé
Rancière, Milner, Badiou

Robert Boncardo
and
Christian R. Gelder

ROWMAN &
LITTLEFIELD
———INTERNATIONAL
London • New York

Published by Rowman & Littlefield International Ltd
Unit A, Whitacre Mews, 26-34 Stannary Street, London SE11 4AB
www.rowmaninternational.com

Rowman & Littlefield International Ltd.is an affiliate of Rowman & Littlefield
4501 Forbes Boulevard, Suite 200, Lanham, Maryland 20706, USA
With additional offices in Boulder, New York, Toronto (Canada), and
Plymouth (UK)
www.rowman.com

© Robert Boncardo and Christian R. Gelder 2017

All rights reserved. No part of this book may be reproduced in any form or by any electronic or mechanical means, including information storage and retrieval systems, without written permission from the publisher, except by a reviewer who may quote passages in a review.

British Library Cataloguing in Publication Data
A catalogue record for this book is available from the British Library

ISBN: HB 978-1-7866-0310-4
    PB 978-1-7866-0311-1

Library of Congress Cataloging-in-Publication Data Available

ISBN: 978-1-78660-310-4 (cloth : alk. paper)
ISBN: 978-1-78660-311-1 (pbk. : alk. paper)
ISBN: 978-1-78660-312-8 (electronic)

∞™ The paper used in this publication meets the minimum requirements of American National Standard for Information Sciences—Permanence of Paper for Printed Library Materials, ANSI/NISO Z39.48-1992.

Printed in the United States of America

Contents

Acknowledgments	vii
Abbreviations	ix
Introduction: The Subject to Which Everything is Attached	1
1 "A Singular Invention of Language and Thought": Jacques Rancière	41
2 "I Believed I Owed Mallarmé the Truth": Jean-Claude Milner	59
3 "Mallarmé Said It All": Alain Badiou	83
Biographies	97
Further Reading	99
Index	107

Acknowledgments

We would like to thank the editors of *Insolubilia*—A.J. Bartlett, Justin Clemens and Jon Roffe—for their advice, their encouragement, their friendship.

Abbreviations

ALAIN BADIOU

AFP	*The Adventure of French Philosophy*
BE	*Being and Event*
C	*Conditions*
HI	*Handbook of Inaesthetics*
IE	*"Is It Exact that All Thought Emits a Throw of Dice?"*
LW	*Logics of Worlds*
ML	*"Mark and Lack"*
MfP	*Manifesto for Philosophy*
NN	*Number and Numbers*
TS	*Theory of the Subject*
TO	*Briefings on Existence: Short Treatise on Transitory Ontology*

STÉPHANE MALLARMÉ

CP	*Collected Poems: A Bilingual Edition*
D	*Divagations*
PV	*The Poems in Verse*

QUENTIN MEILLASSOUX

EP   "Badiou and Mallarmé: The Event and the Perhaps"
NS   The Number and the Siren

JEAN-CLAUDE MILNER

CO   Constats
EVI   Existe-t-il une vie intellectuelle en France?
FLL   For the Love of Language
MP   "Mallarmé Perchance"
MT   Mallarmé au tombeau
NI   Les noms indistincts
OC   L'Œuvre claire
TT   "The Tell-Tale Constellations"
UE   L'Universel en éclats: Court traité politique 3

JACQUES RANCIÈRE

MS   Mute Speech
PL   The Politics of Literature
PS   Mallarmé: The Politics of the Siren

Introduction

The Subject to Which Everything is Attached

> Everything depends on the point of view adopted. This, however, is not only multiple, but indeed, it is only through a succession of points of view, linked one to the other, that any conviction can take form.
>
> —Mallarmé, *Les mots anglais*

This book contains a series of interviews with three major figures in contemporary continental philosophy: Jacques Rancière, Jean-Claude Milner, and Alain Badiou. What unifies this collection is that we ask each thinker to reflect upon their lifelong engagement with the late nineteenth-century poet Stéphane Mallarmé. Rancière, Milner, and Badiou have each been writing since the 1960s and 1970s, and their ideas about the poet can be traced from their earliest publications to the present day. However, what we hope this introduction and the interviews that follow show is that each thinker does not limit himself to commenting on Mallarmé as an historical figure. In fact, their interpretations of the poet intersect with more general debates that have occupied French thinkers for the last half century—debates about the formal distinction between poetic and ordinary language, about literature's relation to the nature and possibility of radical political change, and about poetry's ancient rivalry with mathematics. For the three thinkers interviewed in this collection, Mallarmé's role in twentieth-century philosophy seems to play out a remark the poet himself made about "literary art": that it was the "subject to which everything is attached" (D 195). In the first half of this introduction, we shall examine Rancière, Milner, and Badiou's work on Mallarmé from the perspective of their conceptions of poetic language and mathematics. In the second, we turn to their polemic over the political significance of the poet's work.

MALLARMÉ THE SCIENTIST, MALLARMÉ THE MATHEMATICIAN?

Thanks to his reputation as both a linguistically innovative poet and a theoretician of language in his own right, Mallarmé has long been a privileged object for linguists and literary theorists, not to mention for philosophers concerned with the power of poetry. At the close of her translation of *Divagations* (2009), Barbara Johnson writes that each of Mallarmé's infamous "critical poems is a lesson in how language works." Transcending the limits of a stultifying "communicational language,"[1] Mallarmé's writings show how "[t]he materiality of page, ink, paragraph, and spacing, is often just as important as the logic of syntax, figure, and sense" in the production of linguistic meaning (D 299). For French linguists, from Julia Kristeva to Mitsou Ronat and Jean-Claude Milner, these Mallarméan "lessons" have been key to their creative interventions into the field of a science that has all too often dismissed poetry, delegating it, in Kristeva's words, to "an ornamental place" as an example of the "sacred, the beautiful," or simply "the irrational."[2]

For literary theorists and philosophers, on the other hand, Mallarmé has frequently provided an object lesson in poetry or literature's power. Perhaps because of this, a series of slogan-like formulations have been extracted from their original context, as Thierry Roger has recently lamented.[3] Phrases such as "The pure work implies the disappearance of the poet speaking, who yields the initiative to words..." (D 208); "Words, all by the themselves, light each other up on the sides that are known as the rarest or meaningful only for the spirit..." (D 235); "Verse, which, out of several vocables, makes a total word, entirely new, foreign to the language..." (D 211); "Everything is summed up between Aesthetics and Political Economy..." (D 197), have nevertheless proved sufficiently suggestive as to inspire some of the most exciting literary theory of the twentieth-century. As for philosophy, when Alain Badiou writes that he has long "taken Mallarmé to be emblematic of the relationship between philosophy and poetry" (C 293), his admission seems so universally affirmed that one could be forgiven for thinking it was uttered by either Sartre,[4] Blanchot,[5] Deleuze,[6] Foucault,[7] Lyotard,[8] Campion,[9] or Stanguennec.[10]

More curious still is the long-standing tendency to read some conception of mathematics alongside Mallarmé. As Roger notes, the first Belgian and French reviews of Mallarmé's 1897 masterpiece *Un coup de dés* were mostly concerned with the quasi-mathematical nature of some of the poem's images. He writes, "given its title, the first considerations on the *Coup de dés* were of a philosophico-mathematical order, and not poetic."[11] In addition to the images of a "dice throw" and the "unique Number," references to mathematics are scattered throughout Mallarmé's œuvre, from *Igitur* to "The Book, Spiritual Instrument." In his *Notes sur le langage*, to cite just one instance, he states: "We have not understood Descartes; other countries have taken him over, but he did arouse French mathematicians. We have to take up his momentum, interrogate our mathematicians."[12] Programmatic statements like this sparked the philosophical imagination. Jean Hyppolite, for example, remarks that "attentive" readers of *Un Coup de dés* should look for a point of comparison between the poem and modern mathematics.[13] Similarly, Kristeva and Jacques Derrida brought the insights of late nineteenth and twentieth-century mathematics to bear upon the linguistic subversions they carefully plotted in Mallarmé's poetry.[14] As we shall see, these concerns also motivate the work of Alain Badiou, who not only reads Mallarmé's poetry alongside mathematics, but uses the two to revivify and rethink the Platonic disjunction between poetry and mathematics.

It would be impossible to exhaustively explore these linguistic, literary theoretical, philosophical, and mathematical engagements in this short introduction. To organize the discussion that follows, however, we can begin with the following famous passage from Mallarmé's "Crisis of Verse": "An undeniable desire of my time is to distinguish two kinds of language according to their different attributes: taking the double state of speech—brute and immediate here, there essential." "As opposed to a denominative and representative function," Mallarmé continues, "speech, which is primarily dream and song, recovers, in the Poet's hands, of necessity in an art devoted to fictions, its virtuality" (D 210). All his interpreters provide accounts of the status of this "essential" use of language—this "Verse"—opposed by Mallarmé to what he derides as mere "universal *reportage*" (D 210–211—*modified trans.*). Rancière, Milner, and Badiou are no different. Unsurprisingly given his profession, Milner's early reading of Mallarmé is the most obviously linguistic of the three, as it is inscribed in a problematic born out of the Russian Formalists and their attempt to scientifically define "poetic language" or "literariness."[15] His interpretation of this Mallarméan distinction turns on a Lacan-inspired account of *lalangue*, before taking on a decisively political valence in *Mallarmé au tombeau*, a work published much later in 1999. By contrast, for Badiou, while mathematics pronounces on what is sayable of Being *qua* Being, poetry, exemplarily that of Mallarmé in its search for "a total word, entirely new, foreign to the language" (D 211), names the radically novel event. Before exploring Milner's and Badiou's interpretations in more detail, we must mention that Jacques Rancière's reading is a quite singular case in the history of Mallarmé scholarship, since it neither filters the poet's writings through a linguistic theory, nor draws on them to discuss the differences between mathematics and poetry. To begin this section on linguistics, literature, and science we will therefore deal only briefly with Rancière's Mallarmé, before giving a fuller account in the second section on politics.

JACQUES RANCIÈRE: A NEW EUCHARIST

In an important article on *Mallarmé: The Politics of the Siren* (1996), Alison James remarks on the curious absence of any sustained reflection on poetic form in the book: "In emphasizing [the] triple crisis of verse, ideas and social forms" with which Mallarmé grappled, "Rancière gives surprisingly little weight to the first of these three terms."[16] Compared to the poet's theoretically inclined exegetes like Kristeva,[17] Rancière's reading is indeed characterized by a relative indifference to matters of metre or rhyme, sound or syntax.[18] Moreover, as he states in the interview below, he was not at all concerned with "the great Mallarméan agitation of 1965–70," years during which the poet became the preeminent practitioner of "poetic language," the preferred object of what were then the most avant-garde French linguistic theories. Unlike Milner, Rancière is neither a linguist nor a philosopher of language, despite the centrality he accords to the problematic of *orphaned speech* (MS 46). And yet his indifference to the question of Mallarmé's form is not due to inattention. Rather, a powerful thesis about aesthetic modernity motivates his choice of critical focus. As he writes in *Mute Speech* (1998), the very project of seeking to scientifically describe a distinct "poetic language" or "literariness" misses the fact that "all communication [...] uses signs deriving from a variety of modes of signification: signs that say nothing, signs that efface themselves before their message, signs that have the value of gestures or icons" (MS 63). What is properly modern about Mallarmé's poetry is not its conquest of an intransitive language concerned only with itself. Instead, what truly constitutes Mallarmé's originality—what defines his poetry as such, before and beyond any of its formal characteristics—is the singular task he set himself as a poet; a task he performed, for the most part, with the most traditional images and poetic forms (PS 9).

In a series of books and articles from *The Politics of the Siren* to *Mute Speech*, *The Politics of Literature* (2006) to *Aisthesis* (2011), Rancière shows that this Mallarméan task involves finding a way of solving the central political dilemma of the nineteenth-century: constructing a human community no longer grounded in—nor alienated by—God or an absolute sovereign. "To complete the revolution" of the late eighteenth-century, Rancière writes, nineteenth-century thinkers from the German Romantics to Saint–Simon, Hölderlin to Hugo, believed that "the community need[ed] a new religion" (PS 28). Echoing the results of Bertrand Marchal's seminal *La religion de Mallarmé* (1988), Mallarmé's poetry is thus nothing less than an attempt to create "a new Eucharist, a purely human transformation of the human abode" (PS 16). As a good French atheist, Mallarmé's thinking begins with what he calls his "absolute formula": namely, that "only what is, is" (D 187). In other words, there is nothing beyond the world in its immanence, no "divine denominator of our apotheosis" (D 167), as Mallarmé writes in "Solemnity." Following his famous existential crisis of the years 1866–1869, this lack does not lead him to despair for poetry, which no longer has any transcendental guarantee. Instead, motivated by the conviction that the human being was a "chimerical animal" (PS 30) whose essence lay not in work—*pace* the Saint–Simonians (PS 31–32)—but rather in gratuitous play, Mallarmé uses his poetry to affirm the "glory of that which turns [...] contingency into an unheard-of power of affirmation" (PS 10). By close reading a number of poems and prose pieces, Rancière demonstrates that Mallarmé's writing thus repeatedly transforms mere banalities—a line of foam on a stormy sea, a piece of white linen, a dancing bear—into glorious simulacra—the sign of a vanishing siren-girl, the flight of diving bird, a constellation. For Rancière's Mallarmé, all of these are pure fictions that disappear as soon as they appear for lack of existential solidity. Correlatively, his vision of an ideal community is an evanescent communal incorporation, mediated by a poetic ritual, but one that is immediately disincorporated. Against Wagnerian identitarianism, Mallarmé's "Crowd" is perfectly generic, without predicates.[19] For Rancière, the singularity of his writing does not lie in the formal inventiveness of his poetry or "critical prose". Mallarmé's "essential" language cannot be defined in quasi-scientific terms as either a poetic function or as the primacy of the *semiotic* over the *symbolic*.[20] The essence of his *œuvre* is instead to be found in his overarching political, ethical, and aesthetic vision, itself inscribed in a series of competing nineteenth-century attempts to give expression to humanity's communal essence: "Against the horizontal economic order of trade in merchandise and in words, Mallarmé pits the vertical order of a different economy, a symbolic economy that projects the symbols of common greatness 'at the prohibited elevation of lightning'." (PL 84) We will return to explore this vision at greater length in the second section of this introduction, where we enter the debate over Mallarmé's politics.

JEAN-CLAUDE MILNER: MALLARMÉ BETWEEN GALILEO AND LACAN

With Jean-Claude Milner, we find a far more linguistically informed attempt to describe what he calls "the Mallarméan disjunction" (MT 88) between poetry and "*universal reportage.*" As Kristeva claims in her 1969 essay "Poetry and Negativity," Mallarmé's writings provide professional linguists with a self-conscious example of a linguistic practice that both instantiates the laws they study scientifically and breaks them in a manner that shows the true extent of language's signifying capacities. "Mallarmé," she writes, "was the first to have produced both the theory and practice of this poetic functioning whereby a logic is consistently negated—a logic in which this functioning is nevertheless inscribed."[21] In *Revolution in Poetic Language* (1974), Kristeva exhaustively pursues this hypothesis, drawing on a Lacanian account of subjectivity and her own original concepts of the *symbolic* and the *semiotic* in an effort to describe the kind of linguistic infractions that "texts" like *Un coup de dés* performed with respect to the laws discovered by structural linguistics and generative grammar. Milner's 1978 book *For the Love of Language*, first presented to the Department of Psychoanalysis of Vincennes University in the academic year 1974–1975, is engaged in an almost identical problematic and similarly draws extensively on Mallarmé and Lacan. In his book, however, Milner asks: "What must language be such that it can designate both the object of a science and of a love?" (FLL 64) How, in other words, can language support—and indeed continue to inspire the passionate pursuit of—an indisputably successful science, namely linguistics, at the same time as making up the very matter of poetry?

Mallarmé appears at a number of decisive junctures in *For the Love of Language*. As a poet, he belongs to the diverse group of those Milner names "purists," who he contrasts to linguists (FLL 51, 69–70, 74). The practice of the linguist is motivated by the conviction that the rules that govern language and that allow us to distinguish between the grammatical and ungrammatical are "of the order of the calculable" (FLL 51) and are thus capable of being transcribed by "a symbolic notation" (FLL 68) that supposes their ideal identity. Purists, on the other hand, are partisans of language's exhilarating—but also troubling—tendency to break its own rules via operators such as homophony, homosemy, and homography. More precisely, while purists agree with both grammarians and linguists that language has rules, for them these rules are "nonrepeatable obligations" that are "entirely singular" (FLL 69) and attest to the presence in language of "heterogeneous singularities" (FLL 60) that can never be fully formalized. With language, purists believe, we are privy not only to the inertia of identity, but also to local and fleeting crystallizations of sense, which exploit the capacity of any linguistic unit—letter, phoneme, word, sentence—to be other than it typically is: that is, to actualize the "dimension of the nonidentical" (FLL 58—*modified trans.*). For example, a word whose letters function as an anagram of another (*sirène*, *rien*), or a suite of i's ("les constellations s'initient à briller")[22] whose graphic dimension doubles as a figuration of glinting stars, themselves reinforced by the pinprick of the i's sound. Following the Lacan of Seminar XX and *L'Etourdit*, Milner names *lalangue* this "register which consigns every language to the equivocal" (FLL 61—*modified trans.*).

The paradox of the "purist," however, is that there can be no univocal name for this power of equivocation; no rule for the way language's rules are broken down. The object that sparks their desire is thus by definition "unrepresentable" (FLL 70). Despite the aporetic nature of this desire, Milner's definition of poetry in *For the Love of Language* is precisely that practice which does not give up on representing this unrepresentable: "the act of poetry consists in transcribing in *lalangue* itself and through its own proper channels a point of cessation of the failure [of *lalangue*] to be written" (FLL 74). Referring explicitly to Mallarmé, Milner places his writings alongside other poetic strategies aimed at marking this "point of cessation":

> [...] within the critical tradition, it is easy to identify various names for the point of cessation, a point that could also be called the point of poetry: for one it is death, for another the obscene, for another the purer meaning that is achieved by extracting words from the sphere of ordinary reference—what is called hermeticism. For another, finally, Mallarmé or Saussure, the point at which the lack ceases, the supplement which makes up for it, resides in sound itself, which is thus stripped of what makes it useful for communication; in other words, stripped of the distinctive: no longer the purer meaning, but a multi-faceted homophony. (FLL 74–75—*modified trans.*)

Quoting from "Crisis of Verse," Milner suggests that Mallarmé attempted to transcend the arbitrary nature of the link between signifier and signified—what the poet describes as "the chance that remains between the terms, despite their repeated reformulations between sound and sense" (D 211)—and thus make the phonic qualities of his poetry's "entirely new" words perfectly coincide with the qualities of the objects to which they refer. In this way, Mallarmé writes, verse "makes up for language's deficiencies, as a superior supplement" (D 206).

From one perspective, however, these "deficiencies" are precisely those that arise from *lalangue* itself. Homophony, for instance, is nothing other than a name for the mismatch between sound and sense. As Mallarmé himself famously lamented, "what a disappointment, in front of the perversity that makes *jour* [day] and *nuit* [night], contradictorily, sound dark in the former and light in the latter" (D 205). By the force of equivocity, no language can ever be identical to itself. Indeed, it is not even absolutely clear that a given segment of language belongs to one rather than another: Mallarmé's own penchant for writing simultaneously in French and English attests to this. For Milner, the myth of Babel gives expression to this incessantly heterotopic nature of language, which in turn gives rise to the myth of an "ideal language" (FLL 123) whose subjects would no longer suffer the vertigo of equivocity. Here, Milner again cites Mallarmé's ever-prescient "Crisis of Verse": "Languages [are] imperfect insofar as they are many, the absolute one is lacking" (D 205).

In his 2016 piece "Mallarmé Perchance" Milner reprises this analysis by carefully distinguishing the poet from Saussure. "Mallarmé admits two propositions that Saussure would not accept: first, that the qualities of the phonic form are of consequence; second, that these qualities should, ideally, correspond to the qualities of the thing signified" (MP 87). In contradistinction, then, to Saussure's account of the arbitrary nature of the relation between signifier and signified, Mallarmé thinks "a knowledge" of their relation is indeed "possible" (FLL 96 n. 9). As Milner continues, Mallarmé implies that the subject who is "disappointed" by the contradiction between sound and sense betrays the fact that they had expected an intelligible relation to exist between the two: "Mallarmé [...] assumes that the sonority of the term retains some property of the thing. The examples selected demonstrate that this expectation may be disappointed, but this disappointment, which is accompanied by regret, attests to a promise in which the subject was engaged" (MP 87).

This "promise" is the perfect expression of the purist's desire. Mallarmé's poetry is a practice that nevertheless tries to keep this promise, with the "chance" of language being "conquered word by word" (D 236) in the space of a verse. For Milner, if purists *love* language, as per the title of his book, then it is because language itself promises to compensate for the "deficiencies" it is otherwise responsible for. In *For the Love of Language*, Mallarmé thus stands for a structural position any subject can occupy in language, albeit at the price of an unending oscillation between anticipation and disappointment.

Mallarmé returns in Milner's 1983 book *Les noms indistincts*, a work even more invested in Lacan than *For the Love of Language*. As its title presages, in this book Milner works through a series of categories, some classically philosophical and others more properly linguistic—the Same and the Other, the One, *lalangue*, heteronomy, and synonymy—in order to show how a Real, Symbolic, and Imaginary version of each exists. It is this irreducible tripling of their meaning that ensures their radical equivocity—their *indistinction*. At the close of his fourth chapter on *lalangue*, Milner reads Mallarmé's *Un coup de dés* as a poem that attempts to perform the impossible: to present these three registers of language in their simultaneity. Despite being irreducibly imbricated, the Real, the Symbolic, and the Imaginary are so distinct that each one betrays the other two, absorbing them into its own logic. As Milner has it, "the imaginary imagines only the imaginary, the real exists only by the real, the symbolic writes only the symbolic" (NI 10). However, Mallarmé's *Un coup de dés* comes tantalizingly close to overcoming the impossible and writing all three registers at once:

> [...] in the dry crackle of the two dice, thrown one against the other, one bearing the figure of meaning and the other of sound; in the course of this instant—an instant without duration, but one that, for having taken place once, is such that nothing can make it so that it did not take place: hence the character of an eternal circumstance that, through the alliance of words, can be conferred upon it—we will thus hear the encounter: of S, for it is a matter of numbers (figures of the dices' faces, arithmetic of verse, network of syntax and lexicon), of I, for it is a matter of formed matter (cubes of dice, sonorities and significations of words), of R, finally, the idea of which is given by the cluster of stars, without properties, without any form other an illusion, yet nevertheless countable as the *septuor* and nameable as the *Septentrion* (NI 46).

As previously mentioned, Saussure maintained that there was no intelligible reason for why a given sound or signifier relates to a specific sense or signified: their relation must instead be thought as a "pure encounter" (FLL 88). Milner writes, "the arbitrariness of the sign comes down to positing that it cannot be thought of as other than it is, since there is no reason for its being as it is" (FLL 88). The two dice of *Un coup de dés*—which the Master threatens to throw before disappearing, finally, beneath the waves, with the constellation that appears on the final page representing a successful stellar throw of the dice that doubles the Master's failed throw—are thus said to stage this "pure encounter" of sound and sense. The numbers on the dice represent the purely symbolic nature of the sonic signifier and its corresponding signified. The dice themselves are three-dimensional objects that figure the sensible properties of the Imaginary register. Finally, the stars come as close as possible to figuring the Real, since any sensible form *qua* constellation that emerges against the backdrop of stars is purely illusory and destined to disappear when the vertigo of the infinite reasserts itself. If the dice-throw of *Un coup de dés* occurs in "eternal circumstances," then it is because the "pure encounter" of signifier and signified is at once perfectly accidental, hence circumstantial, yet also necessary—or eternal—since sound and sense will henceforth always be tied together in this specific way. In "Mallarmé Perchance," Milner argues that in a first period of his writings Mallarmé sought to achieve something of a sublation of this contingency—this "Chance"[23]—through the very unit of the verse itself. On Milner's reading, Mallarmé's project of the Book was motivated by the same desire. With *Un coup de dés*, however, if verse is figured as "the cold constellation" (NI 46), then Mallarmé learnt that its apparent victory over Chance is ultimately destined to failure. "The entirety of the *Coup de dés* moreover spells out the failure" of this project, Milner writes—a failure that leads to "the abandonment of the Book" (NI 47). In such a situation, verse can at best be a constellation, which, "for a brief instant, scintillates" (NI 47). Mallarmé thus offers a lesson to those who set off to explore the labyrinth of *lalangue* and its Real, Symbolic, and Imaginary avatars.[24]

Milner's concern in *For the Love of Language* and *Les noms indistincts* with what linguistics can and cannot speak of is the context for his extensive reflections on science since Galileo. From his definitive *Introduction à une science du langage* (1989)[25] to his virtuoso commentary on Lacan in *L'Œuvre claire* (1995), Milner attempts to define the essential features of post-Galilean science, which he believes both structuralist and generativist linguistics participate in. Drawing on the work of the historian of science Alexandre Koyré, Milner highlights the radical historical cut separating two discursive regimes of science: the ancient and the modern, *phusis* and Nature. In Koyré's words, this cut "can be described roughly as bringing forth the destruction of the Cosmos [...] and its replacement by an indefinite and even infinite universe which is bound together by the identity of its fundamental components and laws, and in which all these components are placed on the same level of being."[26] This cut involved Galileo constructing an entirely new vision of science, one that accorded to mathematics a specific and heretofore unprecedented role. As Galileo himself writes, "[p]hilosophy is written in this grand book—I mean the universe—which stands continually open to our gaze, but it cannot be understood unless one first learns to comprehend the language and interpret the character in which it is written. It is written in the language of mathematization."[27] For Milner, the confluence of the new role accorded to mathematics, the advent of the telescope, and the new, infinite Universe allows for a precise understanding of the cut inaugurated by Galilean science; a cut, he claims, that "has not ceased to function since."[28]

Through its "mathematization of the empirical," post-Galilean science inaugurates nothing less than an entire redistribution of the sensible, shifting the nature of the empirical away from qualities accessible to the senses and towards its mathematizable dimensions.[29] But it also places contingency at its center. In the ancient episteme, the function of mathematics and number was to access the Same: the immutable, unchanging laws of Being, hypostatized in a deity. Science today, however, does not confer upon mathematics the same law of necessity. Drawing on Karl Popper's theory of falsification, Milner makes the striking claim that "there is [...] no other science than that of the contingent" (OC 61).[30] This is precisely because modern science is founded on the principle that its theorems and propositions must be falsifiable, and thus that their "referent must be able—logically or materially—to be other than what it is."[31] All the propositions of modern science are therefore nothing but contingencies, able to be other than they are. "Reciprocally," Milner adds, "every contingent can and must be graspable by science."[32] In his commentary on Lacan, Milner notes that the psychoanalyst was himself unaware of Popper's work. Yet he nonetheless recognized that the contingent comprises a key facet of post-Galilean science. Milner writes:

> If one wishes, however, to confine oneself to what Lacan could explicitly think, is it to go beyond the legitimate to evoke Mallarmé here? In truth, if one admits that what is proper to the modern letter is its grasping of the contingent as contingent, the first motto of the age of science states that no letter will ever abolish chance. And the second statement is that every letter is a throw of the dice. The letter is as it is, without any reason causing it to be what it is; by the same token, there is no reason for it to be other than it is. And if it were other than it is, it would solely be another letter. In truth, from the moment that it is, the letter remains and does not change ('the unique number which cannot be another').[33]

Barring the question of the letter here—which, for the sake of brevity, we can simply say is the term Milner uses to characterize the specific languages of modern mathematics[34]—his claim is that Mallarmé anticipated a central aspect of Popper's theory of falsification. However, despite placing the poet directly inside of the post-Galilean lineage in *L'Œuvre claire*, Milner does not think that Mallarmé's poetry can wholly be understood in terms of Galilean science. In fact, in a more recent piece entitled "The Tell-Tale Constellations," he states the opposite.

In this later article, Milner notes that one of the ramifications of the post-Galilean regime concerns the status of constellations: "Constellations do not exist; there only exist the stars that compose them. This is a lemma of modern science. It is also one of the differential traits that separates the *phusis* of the Ancients from post-Galilean Nature" (TT 1). Constellations, while imbued with ideological and cosmological significance, do not have the same status within the post-Galilean regime as they did in the ancient. With the advent of modern physics, stars whose positions can be mathematically mapped are in fact *more real* than the arbitrary groupings of stars comprising the constellations, which exist only from the perspective of an imagining—or, as we shall soon see, *desiring*—observer. It is within the context of this particular problematic that Milner theorizes Mallarmé's relationship not simply to mathematics, but also to modern science in the paradigmatic form of mathematized physics. Given that modern science effects the disappearance of the constellations, Milner examines how nineteenth-century poets confronted this "sacrifice demanded by science." "Among these poets," he writes, "I will distinguish [...] the poets of the sonnet"; and "among these poets of the sonnet I will distinguish Mallarmé" (TT 2).

As we saw before, Milner identifies a doctrine of Chance at work within Mallarmé, which, as he clarifies in "The Tell-Tale Constellations," the poet identifies with the nature of "the Universe [...] insofar as it could be other than it is and insofar as it is as it is." This doctrine works on three levels: the contingent relations between language's sound and sense; the contingent rules of verse; and finally, following the nineteenth-century philosopher of science and religion Émile Boutroux, the contingency of nature's laws.[35] And yet these concerns, for Milner, revolve around something more fundamental: should poetry recognize or ignore the constellations? That is, should poetry renounce or embrace modern science? Citing a line from Mallarmé's 1894 lecture delivered at Oxford and Cambridge, "Music and Letters," Milner writes, "[w]e know Mallarmé's response: Nature has taken place; it cannot be added to" (TT 35). This declaration is nevertheless met in *Un coup de dés* with a response: "NOTHING / WILL HAVE TAKEN PLACE / EXCEPT / PERHAPS / A CONSTELLATION" (CP 142–143). The key feature of this line is that nothing has taken place—that nothing can be added to Nature—except, hypothetically, a fragile point of exception: the constellations. Milner explains that it is "precisely because modern science sanctions their disappearance in the name of Nature [that] it is up to poetry to bear witness to this disappearance, to take note of it definitively so as to constitute it as subtraction and exception" (TT 4). In other words, by attesting to what constitutes an exception to the post-Galilean universe, Mallarmé makes visible what is invisible to modern science. "He maintains," Milner writes, "at the heart of the Universe, the memory of what preceded modern science: the knowledge of the alternations and the constancies of the world" (TT 4). Just as he argued in *Les noms indistincts*, however, the constellations—or indeed verse as such—can appear only for an instant, before they dissolve into the Universe in its formless massivity. "Instead of the Book that had been demanded," Milner writes, the modern poet "retains only the strict desire for Meaning" (NI 47).

While as a poet Mallarmé sits uneasily within the universe of post-Galilean science, taking up an essentially tragic posture defined by alternating acceptance and disavowal, Milner makes it clear that Mallarmé does not abandon mathematics *per se*. Indeed, in his enigmatic *Notes sur le langage*, which Milner cites, Mallarmé affirms: "we must interrogate our mathematicians" (TT 6). However, his is a far older mathematics: the numbers of the constellation *qua* exception are intimately linked to verse, that is, to the rhythmic, syllabic, metrical, and formal calculations that comprise poems. But far from providing a simple return to the ancient episteme, on Milner's reading Mallarmé instead "recalls" (TT 6) the genealogy of number, linking verse to mathematics in a manner that posits a limit—an internal exception—to post-Galilean Nature.

ALAIN BADIOU: THE POEM AND THE MATHEME

Like Milner, Badiou also articulates a relationship between Mallarmé's poetry and mathematics. Developed in his summa *Being and Event* (1988), his ontology and account of the event are in fact organized around a fundamental division between the powers of thought proper to the poem and the matheme. This division puts him at odds with modern philosophers who, from Nietzsche to Heidegger to his French inheritors Lacoue-Labarthe and Nancy, allegedly "sutured" philosophy to poetry, thereby "handing over the whole of thought to *one* generic procedure" (MfP 61). In a conjuncture characterized by the closure of the metaphysics of Presence and the primacy accorded to a linguistically mediated conception of the multiple, poetry, as that which "carries to its highest point language's flexibility and variance" (MfP 42), has understandably been given pride of place. However, one catastrophic consequence of this "philosophical fetishism of the poem" (MfP 87) is the complete voiding of the category of truth. By contrast, Badiou's philosophy is an affirmative attempt to "propos[e], to match the needs of the times, a new step in the history of the category of truth" (MfP 101). For him, truths exist outside of philosophy in the form of four "generic procedures" (MfP 35, BE 16): art, science, politics, and love. While philosophy itself does not produce truth, it must be engaged in a constant dialogue with the generic procedures of its time, opening itself up to the possibility of reworking its own internal operations under the pressure of their unprecedented constructions. For Badiou, Mallarmé is an example of such a generic procedure, having contributed to producing "the truth of French poetry after Hugo" (BE 404). But he is also a poet-thinker of the event: "If I read *Un coup de dés*," Badiou affirms, "then it is as a text of thought, as the greatest theoretical text that exists on the conditions for thinking the event" (IE 74).

But this celebration of Mallarmé's poetic thought is at the same a strict delimitation of its capacities. Against those who confuse poetry with thought *per se*, or who conceive it as thought's highest achievement, Badiou carries out a "Platonic gesture" (MfP 101) that decisively separates poetry and mathematics. While the "flexible availability of language" (MfP 103) in poetry has given it its preeminent place in contemporary thought, for Badiou the "[d]isorientation" occasioned by the modern discovery that "Being is essentially multiple" (MfP 57) can now be integrally "conceptualized" (MfP 74) by mathematics. Thus, in *Being and Event*, the axiomatic succession of ZFC[36] set theory will think Being *qua* pure multiplicity, while poetry will think the event as "that-which-is-not-being-qua-being" (BE 173).

Before we explore how Mallarmé functions as the poet-thinker of the event, it is worthwhile placing this division between poetry and mathematics within the context of Badiou's decades-long attempt to describe and delimit the lines of continuity, similarity, and disjunction that exist between these two discourses. His first attempt to do so occurs in his 1969 article "Mark and Lack," published in the journal *Cahiers pour l'analyse*. Here Badiou makes an early but decisive reference to Mallarmé's relation to mathematics, one that seems to both anticipate and work against how he treats the poet in *Being and Event*. "Mark and Lack" was published in response to Jacques-Alain Miller's influential article "Suture (Elements of the Logic of the Signifier)." Miller's main concern in this article lies in marking out a general structural logic which conditions, produces, and describes every type of structure and "should be conceived of as the logic of the origin of logic."[37] To do this, Miller performs a heterodox reading of Gottlob Frege's logical and metamathematical number theory. For Frege, the essence of number cannot be known in and of itself, and relies instead on a principle of extension that charts a relation between concepts, objects, and numbers. Thus, objects appear as empirically unified only if they are underpinned by their *concept*. Through this relation of the concept to the object, Frege then defines numbers as an extension of this principle: the number representing the concept F is defined as that which is identical to the concept F.[38]

Miller's critique of Frege focuses on the way he treats the concept of the nothing. The number zero is conceptually underpinned by nothing, which makes it the sole number that does not have an object to which it could be identical. Nevertheless, Frege insists on giving it a definition, arguing that the numerical nothing is that which is *not* identical to itself. Miller suggests that although Frege gives the zero a place within his discourse, he paradoxically positions it as a *stand-in* for the one, disavowing the lack his discourse had briefly made manifest.

In "Mark and Lack," Badiou explicitly rejects Miller's determination of how formal language works. While he agrees that the logic of suture emerges when an empirical *thing* is necessary to determine a structure's internal operations, he thinks that the production of a formal language occurs via a different process constituted by three different mechanisms: "concatenation," "formation," and "derivation" (ML 165). In his commentary on "Mark and Lack," Tzuchien Tho adds a fourth element: the "systematic level."[39] Concatenation refers simply to the "raw material" of mathematical marks: the tools for writing that mathematics requires. Formation designates the syntactical rules that govern the manipulation of these marks: one must agree, for example, on what a plus sign means so there can be a universally valid iteration of its use "without remainder" or interpretation.[40] The process of derivation allows one to identify a "well-formed expression," such as $1 + 1 = 2$. Finally, the systematic level names the construction of a general model that regulates or underpins all of these operations (for example, the axioms of set theory). Badiou's critique of Miller suggests that he only attends to this fourth level.

In terms of the nothing, then, Badiou is quite clear: "the zero is not *the mark of lack* in a system, but the sign of the *lack of a mark*" (ML 165). For Badiou, mathematical writing is autonomous and self-sufficient—an integrally rule-governed universe with no lack or subject to "suture." Invoking Althusser, Badiou thus concludes that "Science is an Outside without a blind-spot" (ML 172): referring to nothing outside itself and admitting of no internal exception in the form of the subject, mathematics is the *sole* exception to the logic of suture.[41]

Accompanying this proposition is the following footnote, which makes a crucial reference to Mallarmé:

> If one wants to exhibit writing as such, and to excise its author; if one wants to follow Mallarmé in enjoining the written work to occur with neither subject nor Subject, there is a way of doing this that is radical, secular, and exclusive of every other: by entering into the writings of science, whose law consists precisely in this. But when literary writing, delectable no doubt but obviously freighted with the marks of everything it denies, presents itself to us as something standing on its own in the scriptural Outside, we *know* in advance (this is a decidable problem...) that it merely sports the *ideology* of difference, rather than exhibiting its real process. (ML 172 n. 24)

Here, Badiou implicitly draws on two of Mallarmé's previously mentioned remarks: "The pure work implies the disappearance of the poet," and "Words, all by themselves, light each other up." For Badiou, Mallarmé's dream of completely removing the subject from his or her work—and, simultaneously, of removing empirical reference by way of the self-enclosed nature of poetic writing—recalls the way mathematics also operates. And yet, due to the problems of iteration and interpretation that haunt natural language, it is in fact mathematics—and mathematics alone—that fulfills the ambitions of Mallarmé's dream. For Badiou, what Mallarmé desires, mathematics completes.

When reflecting on "Mark and Lack" in his interview, Badiou suggests that not only did Mallarmé design his poetry with the rigor usually accorded to mathematics, he "also assumed the power of Chance, something mathematics cannot do." This remark allows us to pinpoint the shift between Badiou's early thesis about Mallarmé's relation—or nonrelation—to mathematics and his later work. Whereas, in "Mark and Lack" Mallarmé's work ultimately fails at the task it sets itself, in *Being and Event*, the nonrelation between Mallarmé and mathematics is rendered in positive terms. In a word, Mallarmé is the poet who says—or thinks—that which cannot be said or thought in either ordinary language or pure mathematics, and which corresponds conceptually to Chance: the event.

To understand Mallarmé's role in *Being and Event*, a brief gloss of the theoretical gambits involved in Badiou's 1988 philosophical masterpiece are required. In the book's introduction, Badiou reflects on his early view of mathematics, a time we could easily see as contemporaneous with "Mark and Lack." He writes, "without noticing it, I had been caught in the grip of a logicist thesis which holds that the necessity of logico-mathematical statements is formal due to their complete eradication of any effect of sense, and that in any case there is no cause to investigate what these statements account for, outside of their own consistency" (BE 5). In breaking with this thesis, Badiou first decides axiomatically that Being *qua* Being is pure multiplicity; secondly, he demonstrates that mathematical set theory—a foundational paradigm of pure mathematics introduced by Georg Cantor in the late nineteenth-century—is the sole discourse capable of inscribing pure multiplicity by virtue of the fact that its primitive operation of belonging operates solely on sets *qua* multiples, and never on a One. "I then arrived at the certainty," Badiou states, "that it was necessary to posit that mathematics writes that which, of being itself, is pronounceable in the field of a pure theory of the Multiple" (BE 5). Mathematics is ontology.

While mathematics *says it all* of what is sayable of Being, the role of mathematics only makes up half of Badiou's text. Indeed, although the axioms of set theory are transliterated by Badiou into ontological propositions, there is also a point at which mathematics reaches its own internal limit, its own impasse. Set-theoretical mathematics demonstrates that the quantitative distance between two subsequent transfinite cardinals is undecidable with respect to set theory's own internal rules and operations. This, for Badiou, illustrates that there exists an errancy to being, and, in turn, that radically transformative events are possible; events not calculable, decidable, identifiable, or predictable by means of any established knowledge or recognized linguistic currency.

It is at this point that Badiou turns to poetry. Invoking Mallarmé's famous distinction between an "essential" and a "brute and immediate" use of language mentioned above, he writes: "If poetry is an essential use of language, it is not because it is able to devote the latter to Presence; on the contrary, it is because it trains language to the paradoxical function of maintaining that which, as radically singular, pure action, would otherwise fall back into the nullity of place" (BE 192). Poetry, in other words, names the event. For Badiou, this is a general thesis that holds for all exemplary poetry of the "Age of Poets" (MfP 69–77). According to him, the great achievement of these poets, from Rimbaud to Mallarmé, was to have abolished the category of the object.[42] If an object is that which can be discerned by the knowledge of a given situation, then poetry, "through its sabotage of the law of nominations" (BE 19), is the sole discourse capable of gesturing beyond knowledge to that which ruptures with it, namely the event, and which thus exposes the inconsistency of Being underlying all objectivity. Indeed, just like set-theoretical mathematics, modern poetry motivates us to affirm the nonbeing of the One: "for all the poets of the Age of Poets," Badiou writes, "if the consistency of experience is bound to objectivity [...] it must be audaciously defended that being inconsists" (BE 19). Poetry is thus an essential counterpart to mathematics in *Being and Event*, providing the linguistic means required to hold onto what would otherwise be entirely evanescent and unthinkable.[43]

Mallarmé occupies a singular position in this "Age," however, as he is the poet who explores in the most exhaustive and self-conscious manner the nature of the event. With painstaking precision, Badiou tracks Mallarmé's thought of the event through close readings of a very select number of poems. For instance, he shows how in "À la nue accablante tu" Mallarmé inscribes two very different forms of negation, vanishing and cancellation, which together mark the intrinsic undecidability of the event. First, a hypothetical shipwreck disappears beneath the waves. Then, this vanishing term itself vanishes, with the poem suggesting a second absent cause for the thread of foam that lies on the surface of the sea: a diving siren. This second operator of cancellation then "proceeds to abolish the abolished"—that is, the shipwreck—"and thus mark the undecidability of the event by means of a scission that cancels [the first] hypothesis" (C 52–53). In his reading of the Sonnet en -yx, Badiou again locates the operators of vanishing and cancellation. This time they take the form, on the one hand, of a glint of dying sunlight illuminating a troupe of "unicorns kicking fire against a nixe" (PV 165) in the frame of a dark mirror, and on the other of a constellation that rises, finally, in the mirror's depths. Yet he also pinpoints a third operation, that of foreclosure, which inscribes the absence of any trace of a vanished event, thereby offering up the concept of the "unnameable" (C 55). With "Prose (pour des Esseintes)," Badiou believes that Mallarmé introduces two further operations, separation and isolation, which present a topological figuration of a generic multiplicity, the ontological schema of a truth as developed in *Being and Event*. As Badiou explains, the island to which the poet and his feminine "unconscious" voyage is "separated" from "any possible empirical configuration" (C 65)—that is, from any possible knowledge. The island's flowers—which, as the poet describes them, are "All so immense that each one / ordinarily paraded / in a lucid contour, lacunas se- / parating it from the gardens"—figure the operation of "isolation." As such, they stand for truth in the guise of what remains unknown to "The era of authority" and the "Spirit of litigation"; or, as Badiou names them, "the realists and the naturalists" C 66). Finally, with his long and detailed reading of "L'Après-midi d'un faune," Badiou tracks the stages of a drama of fidelity—and, ultimately, of infidelity—in relation to a vanished event, the poem articulating a series of ideal "temptations" that the Faun-protagonist undergoes in the aftermath of the two nymphs' vanishing (HI 139–141).

Yet, it is Badiou's reading of *Un coup de dés* in "Meditation Nineteen" of *Being and Event* that crowns his mature engagement with Mallarmé. As Jean-François Lyotard acknowledges, Badiou's interpretation is "a very beautiful reading, perhaps the best that has ever been made of the *Coup de dés*."[44] Beginning with Mallarmé's evocation of a vanished shipwreck whose hypothetical disappearance haunts the sea-sky Abyss, Badiou translates this topological configuration of the poem into ontological terms: the Abyss is nothing less than an "eventful site" (BE 175), meaning that the multiples belonging to it—the hypothetical flotsam and jetsam of the shipwreck—are "unpresentable" (BE 194) from the perspective of the situation in which the "eventful site" is presented. Amongst these "allusive debris" (BE 193) is the equally hypothetical Master, whose hand is raised defiantly above the waves, holding a pair of dice he hesitates to throw upon the water. Not only, then, do the dice belong to those "unpresentable" multiples composing the event, the dice throw itself "symbolizes the event in general; that is, that which is purely hazardous, and which cannot be inferred from the situation, yet which is nevertheless a fixed multiple, a number, that nothing can modify once it has laid out the sum—'refolded the division'—of its visible faces." Badiou continues: "A cast of dice joins the emblem of chance to that of necessity, the erratic multiple of the event to the legible retroaction of the count. The event in question in *Un coup de dés* is therefore that of the production of an absolute symbol of the event" (BE 193). Given that the event is strictly "undecidable"—the event can only be decided *as such* once its consequences have been unfolded in the production of a truth—Mallarmé never shows the Master throw the dice. Badiou explains: "Since the master must produce the absolute event [...], he must suspend this production from a hesitation which is itself absolute" (BE 193). We are therefore privy to "a hesitation as eternal as the circumstances" (BE 193).

Badiou then tracks a series of similar figures of hesitation, writing that "the entire central section of *Un coup de dés* organizes a stupefying series of metaphorical translations around the theme of the undecidable" (BE 193). Running concurrently to this series is what Badiou calls Mallarmé's "abstract lesson," namely: "If [...] it were the number, it would be chance." He translates this as follows: "If the event delivered the fixed finitude of the one-multiple that it is, this would in no way entail one having been able to rationally decide upon its relation to the situation" (BE 193). The contingency of the event, in other words, is absolute.

The appearance of the constellation on the final page of the poem—which, the poet clarifies, only "PERHAPS" takes place—constitutes the *second* symbol of the event in the poem after the never-accomplished throw of dice. As Badiou continues, the star's emergence shares with the event the property of the absolute contingency of its occurrence—they emerge "beyond every possible calculation" (BE 193)—and arise here as "compensation" for the "courage required for maintaining the equivalence of gesture and nongesture—thereby risking abolishment within the site" (BE 193). Following Gardner Davies' reading,[45] Badiou claims that if the constellation emerges, then it is because the poem victoriously stages the event in the purity of its concept. "All thought," Mallarmé writes, "emits a throw of dice"; and it is insofar as "a throw of dice will never abolish chance" that Badiou arrives at what he thinks is the poem's maxim, as well as the point at which his philosophy is most truly under the poetic condition. In Badiou's system, while mathematics describes the laws of being, it is Mallarmé who shows us how to "decide from the standpoint of the undecidable" (BE 197)—something mathematics cannot do.

In *Being and Event* Mallarmé's relation to mathematics is thus one of pure disjunction. And yet Badiou elsewhere recognizes an intellectual proximity between Mallarmé and Cantor. Whereas for Milner, the poet stands both inside and outside the Universe of Galilean physics, for Badiou Mallarmé is as radical in his modernity as the founder of modern set theory and the theory of the transfinite. As Badiou writes in *Short Treatise on Transitory Ontology*, Mallarmé is "Cantor's unconscious contemporary" since both poet and mathematician "make of the infinite a number" (TO 124). There is Cantor's transfinite on the one hand, and Mallarmé's "unique Number" (CP 143), that of infinite chance, on the other. While Badiou does not conflate the specificities of either infinite, it is important to highlight that for him, Mallarmé and Cantor participate in the same universe of thought, one where a positive, nontheological articulation of the infinite becomes intelligible. It is here that Badiou positions Mallarmé within a larger lineage, one defined more by mathematics than poetry. Contra Milner, where Mallarmé is seen to draw on mathematics as an exception to post-Galilean mathematized science, in his interview Badiou affirms the following: "Galileo, Newton, Cantor, Mallarmé: for them all, it is a question of authorizing, finally, against the nihilist restriction that is the cult of finitude, and even beyond any God, that the infinite *is*."

COMRADE MALLARMÉ?

The three philosophers interviewed here have all also engaged extensively with the political significance of Mallarmé's writings. In this, they form part of a tradition that has a much longer history in France. From Mallarmé's contemporaries, who debated whether his poetry and personal allegiances meant he was an anarchist or an aristocrat[46]; to his great disciple Paul Valéry, for whom the poet's famed intransigence made him a hero of ethical resistance to the violence and vacuity of modern life[47]; to Jean-Paul Sartre, who took Mallarmé to be the high priest of a dangerously elitist tendency in French letters[48]; to, perhaps most emblematically, the journals *Tel Quel* and *Change*, who during the 1960s and 70s jousted over the political significance of Mallarmé's linguistic innovations,[49] the poet's politics have long been the subject of fiery and extraordinarily polarized debate.[50] Was Mallarmé's isolation from the public sphere a sign of his ethical heroism or of aristocratic disdain for democratic modernity, for example? Were his linguistic inventions the herald of a freer sociality for all speaking subjects or did they destroy the democratic basis for communication? Was his poetry destined for a narrow corporation of his elitist peers or did he truly address it to a generic humanity? Badiou, Milner, and Rancière all write in the force field of these questions, and their responses are equally polarized. To explore this conflict of interpretation, we shall begin by looking at Alain Badiou's *Theory of the Subject* (1982).

ALAIN BADIOU: MALLARMÉ, POET OF THE STRUCTURAL DIALECTIC

First presented as a series of seminars between 1975 and 1979 at Vincennes University, *Theory of the Subject* constitutes the philosophical systematization of Badiou's Maoist political engagement. As a decisive figure in this attempt to revitalize Marxism and dialectical thought, Mallarmé is placed alongside Hegel and Lacan as an exemplary thinker of the so-called structural dialectic, which Badiou aims to integrate and surpass in the direction of the historical dialectic, a form of thought finally adequate to revolutionary change. Thus, while Badiou refers to Mallarmé in a contemporaneous text as nothing less than "the only productive Hegelian of our dominant national tradition of thought" (AFP 12), Mallarmé's dialectic is vital, yet insufficient, to the Maoist militant.

Drawing on a distinction between two figures of the "masses," Badiou claims that Mallarmé was "strongly aware" that the masses who *make* history—as opposed to those who *are* history—"hold the silent secret of any art worthy of its name" (TOTS 65—*modified trans.*). In other words, Mallarmé conceived the generative power of his poetry as nothing less than the "collective grandeur" (TOTS 66—*modified trans.*) of the "seething and destructive masses of the Revolution" (TOTS 67). Badiou focuses on episodes in Mallarmé's writings where the poet stages the "crowd" at festivals explicitly commemorating "the foundational riot": the taking of the Bastille. Commenting on Mallarmé's tribute to fellow poet Villiers de l'Isle-Adam, Badiou points out how for Mallarmé the fireworks of the July 14 celebrations echo in their noise and brilliance the collective's power for revolution, even if the spectators are currently in a state of "self-estranged amazement" (TOTS 67) with respect to their true political capacities. Only the illuminating power of the poem can preserve and reveal the revolutionary capacity of the French people, surrounded as they are by the corrupt parliamentary mediocrities of the Third Republic. For Badiou, Mallarmé therefore occupies a position analogous to that of a militant leader, who similarly enlightens the people to their political potential. By virtue of this perceived analogy, Badiou thus draws on the poet in *Theory of the Subject* to articulate his own political problematic in the wake of May '68 and the fading fortunes of French Maoism.

Yet Badiou also uses Mallarmé to mark a critical line of distinction between appropriate and inappropriate forms of political thought and action. Conceptually, this division runs between the "structural" and "historical" dialectics (TOTS 24–25). In a bravura reading of "À la nue accablante tu,"[51] which differs in intriguing ways from his reading in *Conditions*, Badiou locates Mallarmé's poetic inscription of the logical moves of the structural dialectic. Beginning with the "abyss" in which sea and sky are indistinguishable, Badiou interprets this as a figuration of the concept of the *splace*, but also as a metaphor for the poet's white page. Against this crushingly bleak backdrop, however, the poem also presents "a trace, the foam, [which] holds the principle of a meaning" (TOTS 77) that the foam nevertheless refuses to offer up. Thus, upon the blank page, the poet has placed a thin thread of ink; and in the homogeneity of the *splace*, a mark of something heterogeneous—or, as Badiou puts it, a mark of "strong difference" (TOTS 88)—has fleetingly appeared.

Badiou then states that the poem is about the interrogation of this mark of minimal difference: is the foam the sign of a shipwreck or a siren's dive? As if Mallarmé wanted to reinforce their absence, Badiou notes that he only evokes these two vanishing terms via metonymy (TOTS 72). Conceptually, these metonymic chains, or "weak differences," correspond to the form of causality proper to the structural dialectic, with the shipwreck and the siren constituting their "absent cause" (TOTS 71). Badiou therefore confidently announces that Mallarmé inscribes all the key categories of the structural dialectic. Yet he does so in a way that falsely presents the structural dialectic as the absolute horizon of thought and action. When the first metonymic chain caused by the vanishing shipwreck is annulled by the alternative posited at the shift from the quatrains to the tercets—"or else"—Badiou claims that "strong difference," which had hitherto been repressed by the metonymic "weak differences," momentarily "takes its revenge" (TOTS 88). Yet by immediately proposing a second vanishing term—the siren—Mallarmé reestablishes a second chain of "weak differences." Badiou argues that the very punctuality of this "caesura" (TOTS 88) is part of a conscious strategy: "Oh, but Mallarmé would much rather not show this subject that the structural will of his dialectic stumbles up against! If only all this could be kept within the homogeneity of the poetic operations!" (TOTS 88) Thus, despite recognizing the existence of strong difference, which for Badiou grounds the possibility of revolutionary breaks, Mallarmé filters it immediately into a web of weak differences, whose primacy he thereby attempts to assert. The structural dialectic prevails over the historical dialectic.

In *Theory of the Subject*, Mallarmé is therefore a liminal figure whose brilliant dialectical inventions must be integrated yet surpassed, lest the Maoist philosopher fall short of full revolutionary radicality. In fact, it is only with *Being and Event*—or, just before it, with the essay "Is it Exact that All Thought Emits a Throw of Dice?" (1985)—that the philosopher finds in Mallarmé the resources he needs for thinking, rather than repressing, the event.

JEAN-CLAUDE MILNER: THE POET WHO SHOULD DIE

For Jean-Claude Milner, this show of solidarity between Maoist militancy and late nineteenth-century poetry flies in the face of everything Mallarmé ever thought, wrote, or did. Milner develops his revisionist interpretation out of a clinically precise reading of the sonnet "Le vierge, le vivace et le bel aujourd'hui," which opens as follows:

> The virginal, enduring, beautiful today
> will a drunken beat of its wing break us
> this hard, forgotten lake haunted under frost
> by the transparent glacier of unfled flights! (PV 164)

For Milner, this joyful, exclamative discourse is in fact spoken—or rather silently dreamed—by the immobile, slumbering swan of the second quatrain:

> A swan of old remembers it is he
> magnificent but who without hope frees himself
> for never having sung a place to live
> when the boredom of sterile winter was resplendent.

As Milner explains, the "swan, who was speaking in the first person, brutally interrupts himself in his exclamation of blissful hope because he remembers all of the times where he saw that he could deliver only himself, and where he saw that every effort of general liberation was made in vain" (MT 26). While the first quatrain is purposefully constructed as if it were written by Victor Hugo, or indeed by any Romantic poet exclaiming the promise of "Progress, Liberty, Humanity" (MT 63), it retroactively becomes a mute dream discourse infused with illusory desire. Not only has the poet-swan failed to deliver collective emancipation, his own flights, which he now takes "without hope," have left him stuck in the "boredom of sterile winter." This realization is reinforced in the first tercet:

> His whole neck will shake off this white death-throe
> inflicted by space on the bird denying it,
> but not the horror of soil where the feathers are caught.

If all collective and, ultimately, all individual deliverance are impossible, then the swan must content himself with a pathetic shake of the neck, which at least allows the ice crystals to fall momentarily. However, his wings remain eternally caught in the ice, now revealed to be covering not a lake but dirt. For Milner, these two actions—a wing beat, a shake of the neck—correspond to the poetic doctrines of Mallarmé's two most important predecessors, Hugo and Charles Baudelaire: "First doctrine: a verse is a drunken wing beat, which breaks the chains for an instant. Second doctrine: a verse is a shake of the neck, which is capable, given the impossibility of deliverance, of making the crystals fall one by one" (MT 36). Thanks to its intertextual link with Baudelaire's poem "Le vierge, le vivace et le bel aujourd'hui" allows Mallarmé to articulate his predecessors' doctrines. Following Dolf Œhler,[52] Milner reads "Le Cygne" as illustrative of Baudelaire's own poetic doctrine in contradistinction to Hugo's. Indeed, Baudelaire dedicated his poem to the author of *La Légende des siècles*, who was at that point exiled in Guernsey, hoping thereby to signify that their disagreement over June 1848 was now inessential relative to their shared opposition to the reign of Napoleon III. "Separated politically over June," Milner writes, "the oppression of the Empire brings them together in a common mourning: that of the liberty of all" (MT 51). While Hugo remained a Romantic prophet still pursuing his communitarian dreams, Baudelaire is the melancholy veteran of the June days, whose bloody violence disabused him of the idea that emancipation could ever come, at least in *this* world. "But no matter," Milner says, "each of them believes and knows that the other believes that there is some day"—some "beautiful today"—"for freedom" (MT 51).

Mallarmé opposes both of them. Against almost the entirety of the critical tradition, Milner argues that Mallarmé's infamous "impotence," which he suffered during his years of exile teaching in Avignon and Tournon, was not a function of a young poet's anxiety of influence. Rather, it was Hugo and Baudelaire that were impotent:

> By saying *we* and by speaking of deliverance, it necessarily followed that the Poet had only one task: to sing of a place to live. Yet it sufficed to say *we* and to speak of deliverance for the Poet to reveal himself to be irremediably impotent in accomplishing the only mission that he had been assigned—or more precisely, that he had assigned himself. (MT 53)

According to Mallarmé, Hugo and Baudelaire—that is, modern French poetry *as such*—had been invested with absolutely exorbitant ambitions; it was thus inevitable that they failed to live up to them. Worse, his predecessors linked these ambitions to the existence of revolutions—to some decisive day of deliverance. But for Milner's Mallarmé, there simply "are no marvelous clouds," no unknown outside-of-the-world. There is only this place here below, where the poet can be nothing other than "the phantom of himself" (MT 54). This brings us to the final tercet:

> Phantom assigned to this place by pure brilliance,
> he is paralysed in the cold dream of contempt
> put on in useless exile by the Swan.

If Hugo was the swan of "Le Cygne", "ridiculous and sublime," and if Baudelaire was the mournful figure of Andromache, then Mallarmé is this ultimate figure of the swan, "paralysed in the cold dream of contempt." Hugo was wrong to believe in deliverance, which doesn't exist, and Baudelaire was wrong to mourn its immanent impossibility. The only action left for the poet to perform, as the French original has it, is to "immobilize himself": *Il s'immobilise*. The truth of modernity, for Mallarmé, is not the triumphant march towards emancipation, but rather the infinite extension of a commodity society. Referring to Mallarmé's short-lived fashion journal *La Dernière Mode*, which he believes tracked the installation of this society, Milner argues that for the poet, the nineteenth-century was characterized by "general glaciation, indistinction of beings underneath monochromatic frost, material splendor, and spiritual sterility" (MT 42). Nothing takes place, for Mallarme—nothing but the infinite progression of days, each of which is as anonymous as the previous.

But what of Mallarmé's project of the Book, which was indisputably an attempt to produce a form of gathering that would bring together a community split asunder by the abstract social relations instituted by the state and the market? In *Mallarmé au tombeau*, Milner characterizes the Book as an "institution of perpetual reading and speaking" (MT 79), a description clarified and deepened in "Mallarmé Perchance," where he admits that "the Book was conceived as a means of organizing a multiplicity" (MP 97) of speaking beings and thus of annulling the chance inherent in linguistic encounters between speaking subjects. Milner goes further, likening the Book to what is perhaps the preeminent modern political invention:

> In the end, I would dare to suppose that through the repeated action of the Book, the analogue to a revolutionary party would come into being. The analogy seems more fertile to me than the ceremonial of an atheist religion, too often evoked by commentators. After all, revolution undertakes to abolish the chance that, in society, slots someone or other into the class of the powerful or the class of the poor. (MP 97)

Does Milner therefore accept that Mallarmé's project was continuous with an emancipatory politics? Yes and no. As Milner explains, Mallarmé ultimately concluded—and notably did so after the death of his son Anatole—that, quite simply, chance could not be abolished. This is the "doctrine of the *Coup de dés*" (MT 78), which reprises the "political nihilism" (MP 105) of "Le vierge, le vivace et le bel aujourd'hui." The *Coup de dés*, like "The Demon of Analogy" and the swan sonnet before it, thus articulates a doctrine of poetry that places it at an infinite distance from the world of *ennui*. Reciprocally, it deems all that is not poetry to be insignificant. Poetry itself is the "constellation cold with forgetfulness and desuetude" that the *Coup de dés* announces has perhaps arisen on its final double page. It is the sole exception to the infinite scattering of anonymous events that occur in the here below.

While Badiou consistently confuses his own voice with Mallarmé's, particularly in his post-*Being and Event* work, Milner is concerned to do nothing less with his book than to leave Mallarmé *au tombeau, in the tomb*. Written at the close of the twentieth-century—the "time of the epilogue" (MT 85), as Milner has it[53]—the aim of *Mallarmé au tombeau* is partly to analyze and evaluate the previous two centuries of revolutionary politics, and indeed to reject those of its tendencies that Milner judges to be harmful. Poets are not exempt from his judgment: "Aragon, Neruda, Brecht, etc., the names of criminals" (MT 86). But didn't Mallarmé refuse, on Milner's own reading, the union of Action and Dream? Yes. Yet as Milner goes on to explain, if one reads Mallarmé in "a negative theological mode" (MT 86), his uncompromising commitment to a poetry situated at an infinite distance from the real provides the perfect model for an even purer revolution. Political nihilism and revolutionary idealism thus meet at a common infinite point, which they summon the real to attain. Yet given the inevitable failure of the real to live up to this ideal, both nihilists and revolutionaries can then treat it with contempt. For Milner, this is sufficient reason to break with this *political vision of the world* once and for all.[54]

JACQUES RANCIÈRE: THE PARADOX OF THE DROWNED SIREN

There are few readings of Mallarmé so starkly opposed to Milner's as Jacques Rancière's. For Rancière, Mallarmé was not a nihilist, at least not in the mature and most significant period of his work. Rather, as we mentioned above, he was a poet who took up what Rancière considers the key task of the nineteenth-century: "the creation of a new religion and a new mythology for the people" (PS 28) as a means of completing—or, in a counter-revolutionary mode, of compensating for—the political revolution that had occurred at the close of the eighteenth-century. Mallarmé not only participates in this project; he in fact proposes that his poetry is the sole art form capable of achieving it. In contrast to Milner, Rancière reads "Le vierge, le vivace et le bel aujourd'hui" not as the expression of a doctrine, but rather as a warning regarding the creative impotence awaiting any poet who gives himself an "inaccessible model" (PS 18), an Absolute that poetry seeks but which it can only fall short of. For Rancière, Mallarmé moved beyond this conflict between "the Absolute and Nothingness" (PS 17), a journey he traces in the early poem "Las de l'amer repos." Here, Mallarmé expresses his desire to "have done with the voracious Art / of a cruel land" (PV 39), which imposed upon him the excruciating duty of creating a pure poetry, image of the Absolute. Leaving this "cruel land" behind, Mallarmé takes for his mature poetic model a Chinese jade artist who does nothing more than paint a "pale, thin line of blue" on his cups—a line that could nevertheless "be a lake, set in the sky of naked china," or "a crescent moon eclipsed by cloud." Reprising a distinction that Mallarmé himself evokes, this poetic treatment of a mere "line" is guided, Rancière believes, by the distinction between "the infinite and nothing" (PS 4). Instead of the debilitating dualism of the Absolute and Nothingness, the poetic mobilization of this second distinction involves the fleeting transformation of an everyday "nothing"—a mere line—into a glorious simulacrum of something else entirely, a "lake" or a "moon." The line becomes "infinite" in a dialectical sense, since poetry allows it to cross the limit of its banal, determinate identity, even if it always risks falling back into its status as a mere "nothing."

Rancière thus argues that Mallarmé's mature poetics is an aesthetics of artifice. Most importantly, however, and *pace* Milner, this aesthetics is not a mechanism by which poetry demonstrates its aristocratic distance from the real. Rather, Mallarmé links it to a conception of the essence of the human being as a "chimerical animal" (PS 30) capable of creating fictions without any divinity guaranteeing their existence. Mallarmé's poetry is thereby intrinsically linked to a specific conception of the human collective: it instantiates a power that *all* people are capable of by right. If the people are alienated by the cold modern abstractions of the state and market, then it is because these powers do not recognize their pure capacity for play.

To illustrate this aesthetics, Rancière draws on Mallarmé's prose piece "An Interrupted Spectacle". Here, a bear being exhibited to an audience of workers and petty bourgeois suddenly assumes the posture of a human being, simultaneously suggesting the constellation Ursa Major. The animal is idealized, infinitized: it crosses the limits of its everyday identity. At the very same moment "the crowd," Rancière writes, is "summoned to the spectacle of its grandeur" (PS 14). While the banality of the dancing bear reflects back to the audience its own banality, it nevertheless happens that when this very same spectacle is idealized or transubstantiated—when a glimpse of a second, higher theatre is given through the fleeting transformation of the bear into Ursa Major—the crowd suddenly sees a reflection of its "latent grandeur"

(PS 6). However, in the "aesthetic regime of art," whose logic Rancière has systematically mapped, there is a contingent relation between form and content; or, as he puts it in *Mute Speech*, there is an indifferent relation between the "style" and "the subject represented" (MS 50). This means that the poetic act can only ever be "the vanishing tracing of a precarious ideality" (PS 12). As such, nothing guarantees the bear is Ursa Major, the foam the trace of a diving siren, or the line of paint a lake or a moon: their power is the extremely fragile power "to be without reason, to be by artifice" (PS 15).

In the context of democratic modernity, the contingent relation between content and form is exacerbated by the problematic of what Rancière names *orphaned speech*. As he writes in *Mute Speech*, what is irreducibly proper to language is that it "drifts all over the place" and is "incapable of distinguishing whom it should or should not address and so talks to everyone in its mute way" (MS 46). Language essentially confounds all fixed meanings and all relations between a subject and the speech that is proper to them. What this means for Mallarmé is that he can never guarantee that the "new Eucharist" (PS 16) he aims to institute through his poetry will succeed: it always risks being a "dead letter" (PS 22—*modified trans.*). It is not for nothing, then, that in "An Interrupted Spectacle" Mallarmé affirms that the idealization of the bear into the form of a constellation requires "a man habituated to dreaming"[55]—a man capable of perceiving this sign of "collective grandeur" where others see only an occasion for taking fright. The egalitarian address and metaphysics of his poetry, along with its ideal democratic circulation, thus strictly corresponds to a privileging of the poet's position.

Despite this structurally necessary elitist deviation, Rancière registers Mallarmé's opposition to another deleterious political tendency, Wagner's mythology of national origins. In fact, Mallarmé's polemical encounter with the composer of the *gesamtkunstwerk* is of the greatest interest to Rancière, as it intersects with the poet's confrontation with music, the art form that appears to achieve the antirepresentative ideal of the aesthetic regime of art (PS 35–38). As Rancière writes, at the furthest remove from narrative forms in which we witness nothing more than "the simple nothingness of banality looking at itself in the mirror" (PS 36), music is a language purified of representational intent: "The abstract shivers that the writing of notes and intervals confides to the timbre of instruments can thus immediately be transformed into shivers of emotion" (PS 35). Mallarmé is impressed by the way the performance of an orchestra can bring together a community of subjects without imposing any precise *idea* or *identity* that these subjects would all participate in, all the while allowing for the act of idealization that is proof of humanity's "chimerical grandeur" (PS 35).

However, it also brings with it a redoubtable danger. Like Hegel, Mallarmé recognized that the flipside of the antirepresentationalism of music was its tendency to coincide either with the most banal, narcissistic interiority or to be appropriated by those willing to anchor its force to a mythology of origins (PS 38). Mallarmé believes that Wagner effected a fraudulent compromise between the antirepresentationalism of music and a nationalist mythology, chaining the awesome yet indeterminate power of the former to the latter's identitarian limits: "Music, then, is consecrated as the religion of the people, the Eucharist of the real presence to self of a people defined as a community of origins, of a people called itself to become the total work of art" (PS 40). Between the horns of this dilemma—the void of indeterminacy on the one hand, identitarianism on the other—Mallarmé chooses the "intellectual word at its height" (D 210): poetry is the perfect synthesis of music and letters. But is poetry subject to the same dangers that Mallarmé so decisively identifies in other art forms, from the banality of representational theatre, to the unconscious ephemerality of ballet, to the indeterminacy of music? For Rancière, the answer is yes. In a procedure that Rancière names *the circle of mimesis* (PS 48), Mallarmé exteriorizes the immanent fragility of his own poetic operations onto other art forms—a fragility that flows from the contingent relation of form and content. In other words, he cannot consecrate his own art except by using the faults of the others as alibis. Mallarmé treats the other art forms as mere simulacra of the true expression of the creative essence of humanity. Yet those properties that make them simulacra in the first place *are also properties of poetry*. Rancière summarizes this complex movement as follows: "Always, the 'book of verse' springs forth as the true theatre of the spirit, the theatre which imitates only the Idea and of which every other art is a simple imitation. But Mallarmé never managed to conceive this first model, except as the imitation of its imitations" (PS 52). Despite its antirepresentative ambitions, Mallarmé's poetry is indeed mimetic: each of its instantiations must repeat the gesture of idealization. If the *Coup de dés* has a singular place in Mallarmé's *œuvre*, then for Rancière it is because it is the poet's ultimate attempt at authenticating his poetry—at demonstrating its unique capacity to be a "new Eucharist."

But how does this attempt at offering a "proof"[56] (PS 57) play out? Returning to Plato, Rancière argues that given the irreducibility of the problem of *orphaned speech*, no immediate presentation of sense is guaranteed; there is an essential precariousness to any linguistic presentation. For this reason, Mallarmé's writing "is two things at once: it is both text and interpretation" (MS 140). This constitutive scission means that some other mechanism is always in play in order to guarantee the presentation of the intended and determinate sense. While this mechanism is itself submitted to the same rule of *orphaned speech*, its presence is nevertheless called upon as a way of controlling its effects. Rancière gives two examples of such a mechanism: "another type of writing has always had to compensate: one that is less than written, similar to the breath of spirit; one that is more than written, either averred in the body of one who speaks, or etched in the very texture of things" (MS 53—*modified trans.*). In other words, the authenticity of a linguistic presentation can be verified either by saying that it is the materialization of a self-present spirit or mind, or by the position of the person speaking. But as Rancière points out, Mallarmé has recourse to neither of these mechanisms: "The Mallarméan theory of fiction rejects the figures of carnal incorporation and immaterial breath" (MS 53). There is no God, no Platonic *eidos*, and therefore no immaterial "spirit" animating and authenticating the words of his poems. Furthermore, in the aesthetic regime of art, "[n]o writing can designate the rule or the public that testifies for it" (MS 57). And while it may seem that it is the "man habituated to dreaming" who can see the vanishing presence of the Idea in a popular theatre or a ballet performance, this privilege must in principle be extended to *all* in democratic modernity if the poem is to truly "consecrate the community's abode [and] give it the seal of grandeur proper to humanity" (MS 191 n. 24—*modified trans.*). No hierarchical conception of the community can come to the aid of the Mallarméan Idea.

Only one path seems to remain open: the "two figures of another type of writing"—the supplementary writing that comes to bolster the text in its essential precariousness—must "merge in the sole materiality of the book" (PS 53). In its deployment of the material specific to literature— "the white of the open page, [the] unequal lines of characters borrowed from diverse fonts" (PS 53–54)—*Un coup de dés* is guided by the goal of making matter and form coincide without remainder. The materiality of the book, rather than being a superfluous empirical accident attendant upon the ideal passage of sense, paradoxically becomes the sole means for ensuring the production of the Idea. The ideogrammatic dimension of *Un coup de dés* is therefore deployed in order to institute a play of correspondences between what the poem says and what it does or shows, as well as between the idea of which it speaks and the object it claims to imitate.

This full deployment of the capacities of literature is, of course, part of the general movement in artistic modernity towards the assumption of literature's autonomy. Yet this search for autonomy is not about making the work an *absolute* or an end in itself. Rather, this movement of autonomization involves an unavoidable confrontation with other forms of art—theatre, music, ballet—and its goal is the authentic presentation of the community's "latent grandeur." For poetry to assert its autonomy is thus for it to simultaneously assert its authenticity as "the consecration of the human abode."

On Rancière's reading, the *Coup de dés* is the unprecedented product of these intersecting aesthetic and political concerns. The drama it stages of a phantom shipwreck and the series of other hypothetical events which—perhaps—occur on the stormy sea that is its backdrop, is for Rancière essentially the same drama that is played out in the sonnet "À la nue accablante tu." There, if the siren dived beneath the waves, then it was not only because of the necessarily ephemeral nature of the Idea in Mallarmé; it was also because, for a more elitist reason, he believed that his time was not yet ready to hear its song. As we have seen, Rancière demonstrates how in the context of the aesthetic regime of art Mallarmé necessarily oscillates from the egalitarian, indeed emancipatory posture of the poet who produces the "new Eucharist," to a quasi-aristocratic posture by which he denigrates other art forms—and, by extension, those who consume them—as the sole means available to him to authenticate his own poetry.

The play of appearing-disappearing in *Un coup de dés*, for Rancière, therefore derives from both the precarious status of Mallarmé's idealities, and the withdrawal or isolation of his poetry from the swarm of simulacra that are the other competing art forms of his time. This withdrawal is the only defense against *orphaned speech*, the effects of which Mallarmé had discerned in theatre, ballet, and music. Thus, *pace* Jean-François Hamel, who argues that Mallarmé isolates himself from the "crowd" out of a sense of "political prudence,"[57] it is in fact because his utopian designs are infinitely deferred. Never will Mallarmé truly succeed in counteracting *orphaned speech*, and never will he emerge from his aristocratic isolation.

Rancière's Mallarmé thus appears as something of a synthesis of the countervailing tendencies manifested by the poet's specifically political reception: he is both a democrat and an elitist; a seeker of emancipation and an aristocrat who must condemn much of what counts for his contemporaries. Thus as Badiou remarks in his reply to *Mute Speech*, Rancière's reading of Mallarmé validates "an absolutely classic thesis" about the poet: that his work ends in "failure."[58] In other words, *The Politics of the Siren* ends on something of a tragic note, with Rancière showing the unbridgeable gap between Mallarmé's—or modern literature's—political ambitions and the resources it has at its disposal to achieve them.

What we have seen, then, is that for these three thinkers Mallarmé embodies the very descriptor he himself assigned to literary art: "this subject to which everything is attached" (D 195). In the philosophers' hands, Mallarmé the historical figure transforms into a political nihilist, a principled egalitarian, a thinker of the infinite, and a quasi-mathematician. And yet each of these singular images of the poet appears incommensurable with the previous. As scientific, mathematical, and political debates rage in the French philosophical scene, we can nonetheless safely say that Mallarmé's poetry will continue to be placed at their center. In this introduction, we have not attempted to adjudicate these debates, to pick a clear winner. Instead, we hope only to show that they exist, and constitute fundamental lines of fracture between Rancière, Milner, and Badiou. For, after all, whatever position the reader decides to take up, everything that Mallarmé will continue to be attached to still depends on the point of view adopted. But it is precisely these multiple points of view that give rise to the firmest of philosophical conviction.

NOTES

1. Julia Kristeva, "Le texte et sa science," in *Sèméiôtiké: Recherches pour une sémanalyse* (Paris: Editions du Seuil, 1969), 9.

2. "Le texte et sa science," 7.

3. Thierry Roger, "Camarade Mallarmé': mallarmisme, anachronisme, présentisme," Acta fabula, "Réinvestissement, rumeur & récriture," Vol. 15, No. 6 (2014).

4. Jean-Paul Sartre, *Mallarmé, or the Poet of Nothingness*, trans. Ernest Sturm (University Park, PA: Pennsylvania State University Press, 1988).

5. Maurice Blanchot, *Faux Pas*, trans. Charlotte Mandel (Stanford, CA: Stanford University Press, 2001) and Blanchot, *The Book to Come*, trans. Charlotte Mandel (Stanford, CA: Stanford University Press, 2003).

6. Gilles Deleuze, *Nietzsche and Philosophy*, trans. Hugh Tomlinson (New York: Columbia University Press, 1983) and Deleuze, *The Fold: Leibniz and the Baroque*, trans. Tom Conley (London: Continuum, 1993).

7. Michel Foucault, *The Order of Things: An Archaeology of the Human Sciences* (New York, NY: Vintage Books, 1994).

8. Jean-François Lyotard, *Discourse, Figure*, trans. Anthony Hudek and Mary Lydon (Minneapolis, MN: University of Minnesota Press, 2011).

9. Pierre Campion, *Mallarmé, poésie et philosophie* (Paris: PUF, 1994).

10. André Stanguennec, *Mallarmé et l'éthique de la poésie* (Paris: Vrin, 1992).

11. Thierry Roger, *L'Archive du Coup de dés* (Paris: Éditions Classiques Garnier, 2010), 53–54.

12. Mallarmé, *Œuvres complètes I, Edition présentée, établie et annotée par Bertrand Marchal* (Paris: Gallimard, 1998), 872–873. This is Mary Ann Caws' translation. See Stéphane Mallarmé, "Descartes," in *Mallarmé in Prose*, trans. Mary Ann Caws (New York, NY: New Directions, 2001), 76.

13. Jean Hyppolite, "Le Coup de dés de Stéphane Mallarmé et le message," *Les Études philosophiques*, No. 4 (1958), 466.

14. See Julia Kristeva, "Towards a Semiology of Paragrams," in *The Tel Quel Reader*, ed. Patrick French and Roland-François Lack, trans. by Roland-François Lack (New York: Routledge, 1998) 25–49 and Jacques Derrida, "The Double Session," in *Dissemination*, trans. by Barbara Johnson (Chicago, IL: The University of Chicago Press, 1981) 173–286.

15. In addition to *For the Love of Language* and *Les noms indistincts*, see also 'Réflexions sur le fonctionnement du vers français' in *Ordres et raisons de langue* (283–301) and his co-authored book on versifiaction *Dire le vers* (1987).

16. Alison James, "Poetic Form and the Crisis of Community: Revisiting Rancière's Aesthetics," in *Thinking Poetry: Philosophical Approaches to Nineteenth-Century French Poetry*, ed. Joseph Acquisto (London: Palgrave MacMillan, 2013), 169.

17. Kristeva painstakingly maps, for instance, the phonemic patterns of poems like 'Prose (pour des Esseintes)', as well as examines the syntactic structure of *Un coup de dés*. Julia Kristeva, *La révolution du langage poétique: L'avant-garde à la fin du XIXème siècle: Lautréamont et Mallarmé* (Paris: Editions du Seuil, 1974), 239–263, 274–291.

18. For the few exceptions to this rule, see his remarks on the syntax of the sonnet 'A la nue accablante tu', PS 1–3; on the typographical dimension of *Un coup de dés*, PS 53–54; and on the phonic and rhythmic characteristics of a poetry that would seek to imitate music, MS 136.

19. PS 40. See also *La Religion de Mallarmé*, 189.
20. *Revolution in Poetic Language*, 611–612.
21. 'Poetry and Negativity', *op. cit.*, 268.
22. Stéphane Mallarmé, 'Conflit', *Igitur, Divagations, Un coup de dés* (Paris: Gallimard, 2003), 118.
23. "The arbitrary, in this sense, only names the encounter—what Lacan better names contingency, and also what Mallarmé names Chance," FLL 87.
24. Or, as he puts it in *For the Love of Language*, "the *Coup de dés* is a proposition about language," FLL 96 n. 9.
25. Jean-Claude Milner, *Introduction à une science du langage* (Paris: Editions du Seuil, 1989).
26. Alexandre Koyré, *From the Closed World to the Infinite Universe* (Baltimore, MD: The Johns Hopkins Press, 1957), 2.
27. Quoted in Michel Blay, *Reasoning with the Infinite: From the Closed World to the Mathematical Universe*, trans. M. B. DeBevoise (Chicago, IL: The University of Chicago Press 1998), 1.
28. *Introduction à une science du langage*, 21.
29. See Milner's discussion of Saussure in light of this redistribution, FLL 80, n. 6.
30. See Oliver Feltham's partial translation of this work: Jean-Claude Milner, 'The Doctrine of Science,' trans. Oliver Feltham in *Umbr(a): Science and Truth*, No. 1 (2000), 52.
31. *Ibid.*
32. *Ibid* 53.
33. *Ibid.*
34. See his long discussion of the letter in OC 128–132.
35. Émile Boutroux, *The Contingency of the Laws of Nature*, trans. Fred Rothwell (Chicago/London: The Open Court Publishing Company, 1920).
36. The axiomatization of set theory by Ernst Zermelo in 1908 was intended to solve the potentially fatal problems directed towards the discourse at the turn of the century, such as early ideas about Russell's paradox. This consisted in formalising the minimal amount of necessary givens needed to underpin set theory's operations. As Zermelo writes: "I intend to show how the entire theory created by Cantor and Dedekind can be reduced to a few definitions and seven principles, or axioms, which appear to be mutually independent [...] I have not yet been able to prove rigorously that my axioms are consistent, though this is certainly very essential; instead I have had to confine myself to pointing out now and then that the antinomies discovered so far vanish one and all if the principles here proposed are adopted as a basis". Ernst Zermelo, "Investigations in the Foundations of Set Theory 1," in *From Frege to Gödel: A Source Book in Mathematical Logic, 187–1931*, ed. Jean van Heijenoort (Cambridge/Massachusetts/London: Harvard University Press, 1967), 200–1. See also, "Meditation Three" in BE.

37. Jacques-Alain Miller, "Suture (Elements of the Logic of the Signifier)," in *Concept and Form: Volume 1, Key Texts from the Cahiers pour l'Analyse*, ed. Peter Hallward and Knox Peden, trans. Jacqueline Rose (London: Verso, 2012), 92.

38. *Ibid.*

39. Tzuchien Tho, "The Void Just Ain't (What it Used to Be): Void, Infinity, and the Indeterminate," *Filozofski vestnik*, Vol. 34, No. 2 (2013), 40.

40. Tom Eyers, *Post-Rationalism: Psychoanalysis, Epistemology, and Marxism in Post-War France* (London: Bloomsbury, 2013), 32.

41. "By 'logic of the signifier', we mean here the system of concepts through which the articulation of the subject is achieved: Lack, Place, Place-holder, Suture, Foreclosure, Splitting. These concepts have been produced by Jacques Lacan and we acknowledge a definitive debt to him even as we engage in the process that circumscribes their use: this is the critical procedure. The thesis we are defending here aims only at delineating the impossibility of a logic of the signifier that would envelop the scientific order and in which the erasure of the epistemological break would be articulated," ML 160 n. 4.

42. "The fundamental line followed by our poets, which enables them to subtract themselves from the effects of philosophical suture, is the destitution of the category of object. More precisely: the destitution of the category of object and of objectivity as necessary forms of presentation," MfP 72.

43. "This is what Mallarmé tells us: Whoever restores the category of the object, which the even always revokes, is led back to abolition, pure and simple," HI 136.

44. Philippe Lacoue-Labarthe, Jacques Rancière, Jean-François Lyotard, and Alain Badiou, "Liminaire sur l'ouvrage d'Alain Badiou 'L'Être et l'événement," *Le Cahier (Collège international de philosophie)*, No. 8 (1989), 234.

45. Davies also interprets the poem as a conceptual drama, with the upsurge of the constellation being a logical consequence, on Davies' more Hegelian reading, of Mallarmé's synthesis of throwing and not-throwing the dice: "At the philosophical level, the poem is a striking illustration of the logic of contraries. Having concluded with the philosophical identity of contraries, the poet demonstrates that it is possible, by maintaining this equivalence in an implicit state, to transcend it and to arrive at the Absolute [...]; such is the meaning of the appearance of the point of light in the immensity of the black sky," *Vers une explication rationnelle du 'Coup de dés'*, 158.

46. See Thierry Roger's recent work on the contemporary reception of Mallarmé's politics, Thierry Roger, "Art and Anarchy in the Time of Symbolism: Mallarmé and his Literary Group," *S: Journal of the Circle for Lacanian Ideology Critique*, "Mallarmé Today" (2016).

47. See Jean-François Hamel's discussion of Paul Valéry in Jean-François Hamel, *Camarade Mallarmé: Une Politique de la lecture* (Paris: Editions de Minuit, 2014), 44–53.

48. Jean-Paul Sartre, *The Family Idiot. Gustave Flaubert 1821–1857. Volume 5* (Chicago, IL: The University of Chicago Press, 1993), 163.

49. For exemplary texts on Mallarmé by contributors to *Tel Quel* and *Change*, see Jean-Pierre Faye, 'Le camarade Mallarmé', *L'Humanité*, September, 1969 and Philippe Sollers' response, Philippe Sollers, ' "Camarade" et camarade', *L'Humanité*, September 1969.

50. For the best account of this history, see Jean-François Hamel, *Camarade Mallarmé: Une Politique de la lecture, op. cit.*

51. TOTS 74–83, 87–97.

52. See Dolf Œhler, *Le Spleen contre l'oubli: Juin 1848. Baudelaire, Flaubert, Heine, Herzen* (Paris: Payot, 1988).

53. For an English translation of the final chapter of *Mallarmé au tombeau*, see Jean-Claude Milner, "Prose Redeemed," trans. John Cleary, S: *Journal for the Circle of Lacanian Ideology Critique*, Vol 3 (2010): 106–113.

54. See Milner's analysis of this concept in *Constats*.

55. Stéphane Mallarmé, "Villiers de l'Isle-Adam," in *Œuvres complètes, II, Edition présentée, établie et annotée par Bertrand Marchal* (Paris: Gallimard, 1998), 481.

56. For a classic exploration of the notion of "proof" in Mallarmé's *œuvre*, see Jacques Scherer, *Le 'Livre' de Mallarmé* (Paris: Gallimard, 1978), 91–96. For a discussion, see Valérie Jacquod, *Le roman symboliste: un art de l'extrême conscience: Edouard Dujardin, André Gide, Rémy de Gourmont, Marcel Schwob* (Paris: Droz, 2008), 400–406.

57. Jean-François Hamel, Camarade Mallarmé, 179.

58. Alain Badiou, "Autour de La parole muette de Jacques Rancière," Horlieu, Vol. 10, No. 18 (2000), 93.

Chapter One

"A Singular Invention of Language and Thought"

Jacques Rancière

MALLARMÉ, LITERARY HISTORY, AESTHETICS

Robert Boncardo and Christian R. Gelder: From Sartre and Blanchot's post-World War II readings to the deconstructive intervention of Derrida's "The Double Session" to Badiou's more recent engagement with Mallarmé, French thinkers have persistently produced philosophically inflected readings of the poet. During this period, it would seem as though Mallarmé became the emblem of literature's link to philosophy. Can you reflect on the role the poet played in post-war French philosophy?

Jacques Rancière: In fact, it was not as an emblem of the relation between literature and philosophy that Mallarmé became important, but as an emblem of pure literature or pure poetry and of the problematic relation between this purity and political radicality. On the first point, it must be remembered that it was Valéry who had prepared the terrain: it was not for nothing that the group who wanted to make Mallarmé the hero of materialist modernity called itself *Tel Quel*. And it was within a Telquellian context that Derrida addressed Mallarmé. On the second point, it was indeed the Sartrean theme of engagement—and disengagement—that made Mallarmé an exemplary negative case. What Sartre studied was a symbol of a literature that turned away from social reality and devoted itself to its own purity, that is, in fact, to an elitist game. On the contrary, the theoreticians of *Tel Quel*, all the while explicitly reprising Valéry's vocabulary, argued in favour of the concordance between political revolution and the revolution of poetic form. Badiou first addressed Mallarmé as a figure of anxiety, as opposed to the courage of action, before finding in him the exemplary figure of poetry as a truth procedure—a procedure that produces a truth without producing the knowledge of this truth. For my part, if I became interested in Mallarmé, it was to challenge a certain idea of poetic modernity as autotelic.

RB & CG: Your first engagement with Mallarmé occurred once you had already established your place within twentieth-century French philosophy. Did Mallarmé nevertheless play a role in your philosophical education prior to the publication of *Mallarmé: The Politics of the Siren* in 1996? Was he a point of reference during your formative years?

JR: No, Mallarmé did not play a formative role for me. Being young, I read first and foremost the poems he wrote in his youth, which are the least significant. And I did not feel concerned by the great Mallarméan agitation of 1965–70 when *Tel Quel* made him the hero of a poetics of the primacy of the signifier, and waged war against Jean-Pierre Faye over "comrade Mallarmé." I became interested in him in the context of a seminar on the politics of writing I held at the *Collège International de Philosophie* at the beginning of the 1990s. It was at that moment I felt it necessary to criticize the paradigm that had made him a representative of the purity of an autotelic language. I demonstrated, to the contrary, how his poetic project gave poetry an active role at the heart of a community and how it implied a transformation of poetic language on the basis of nonlinguistic forms borrowed from music, dance, or from ceremonies, as well as on the basis of analogies with the movement of waves, the explosion of fireworks, or the movement of fans.

RB & CG: *The Politics of the Siren* was your first work devoted exclusively to literature and aesthetics, and it remains the sole monograph you have written on an individual author. Can you explain the reasons behind your choice to write on Mallarmé at the moment of your turn to aesthetics?

JR: In a sense, the writing of this book was purely accidental. The director of the collection had solicited me and I had proposed to write a book on Flaubert for him. As Flaubert had already been assigned, I took Mallarmé by default. That said, my interest in Mallarmé had nothing to do with an "aesthetic turn." I have always been concerned with aesthetics in a precise sense: that of the relation between bodies, the places, and the temporalities they are assigned, and the words and spectacles that confirm or transgress this assignation. My work on Mallarmé was inscribed in the logic of a work on the politics of writing that I undertook in the 1980s as a prolongation of *Proletarian Nights*— a work that also fed into *On the Shores of Politics* and *The Names of History*. It was a matter of working on the way in which words become flesh or acts, as much in the life of a proletarian who discovers writing as in the life of the monks of the desert, of an English poet discovering the décor of the French Revolution, or of historians confronted by the speech of the poor and heretics. It was over the course of one of my seminars on the politics of writing that I began to address the case of Mallarmé. At the time, he was the great symbol of "autotelic," antirepresentative modernity, and was always placed alongside emblematic figures of a turn towards abstraction in art like Malevitch or Schönberg. It was then that I was able to gauge just how much the project and the writing of Mallarmé were opposed to this dominant *doxa*: Mallarmé gave poetry the social vocation of preparing the celebrations of a community to come, and for this he sought his models in the performing arts. If my work on Mallarmé represented a turn, then it was to the degree that it initiated the larger critique of the modernist paradigm that I went on to produce, notably in *Aisthesis*.

DIFFICULTY, FORM, ELITISM

RB & CG: The descriptor *difficult* has been a recurring trope in the reception of Mallarmé's writings. You yourself have intervened into this debate by strenuously disagreeing with those who, like Chassé and, to a degree, Sartre, see this difficulty as arising from an aristocratic cabalism, one which purposely mystifies an otherwise communicable message. Against this, you insist upon the irreducible imbrication of content and form in Mallarmé's poetry, but also on its universal address. So much so that your book appears to offer an apology for his infamous difficulty, which you come to construe as a direct and proportionate poetic response to the aesthetic and political difficulties of his time. What is at stake for you in the question of Mallarmé's difficulty? How do you understand the relation between the extraordinary complexity of his writings and their egalitarian horizon?

JR: I wanted to challenge a simple opposition between communicative language and the poetics of the incommunicable. Mallarmé belongs to the beginning of an epoch where artists—poets, painters, musicians, dancers, designers or, later, filmmakers…—called into question a certain model of the communication of messages and emotions: that of the story narrated, of events that are linked together, of characters whose feelings we follow, and of the moral that is to be drawn from all of this. This calling into question has often been described as elitist or formalist. But we forget that the displacement towards form or towards performance often took popular spectacles as its models (pantomime, the circus, music hall, fêtes, and, later, sport), and pursued a new alliance with the people on the basis of the very divergence with the bourgeois model of cultural consumption. Think of the way in which the Symbolist theatre directors, abstract painters, or "Cubo–Futurist" artists transformed themselves into militants of the Soviet revolution. Mallarmé is at the beginning of this movement. He finds his inspiration in the "little theatres," in "music hall," and in country fairs. He dreams of a poetry become performance that would "marvel" the people in the way fireworks do during a civic celebration. At the same time, his poetic practice is stretched across a plurality of models: the new and vaguely dreamed of Symbolist theatre, the poem perfectly closed in on itself in the form of a riddle, the idea that has found its typographical equivalent on a page conceived as a theatrical stage, the "current affairs" [*grand fait divers*] that stage the social conditions of the poetic act… Once again, the difficulty is Mallarmé's own before it is that of the reader. It is to define the poetic mode corresponding to what for him seems to be the task of the poet in his time.

RB & CG: When discussing the significance of the "crisis of verse" that shook the French literary field in the late nineteenth century, you contend that this crisis was derivative of the historical novelty of the aesthetic regime of art itself. You argue that there can be no definitive idea of what constitutes poetry in the modern age, since an essential indistinction of the literary and the nonliterary inheres in this regime. The fragility of the category of the literary therefore creates the conditions in which the "crisis of verse" can occur. But is this not to downplay the specifically formal—indeed poetic—stakes of this crisis? While there are doubtless definitional difficulties posed, for instance, by the works of Gustave Kahn and Jules Laforgue when they are compared with poetry written using traditional forms of versification, there still remains a quite discernible distinction between free verse and prose writing—not to mention between free verse and the prose of the world. Does seeing the "crisis of verse" as derivative of a crisis in the idea of the literary more generally not strip the problem that Mallarmé confronted of its properly poetic specificity?

JR: What matters is knowing what we mean by "properly poetic." "Poetry" has always signified much more than the art of writing verse. For Mallarmé, to refuse the solution of free verse is not to refuse a certain form of "poetic specificity" that would tie poetic form to the question of an equal or unequal number of feet. The search for the "number" is precisely the search for a measure of the poem that escapes arithmetical harmonies and disharmonies, a little like how geometrical proportions were tasked by Plato with subtracting the city from simple arithmetical equality. For Mallarmé, poetry's specificity is to be an act of language that belongs to a symbolic economy destined to consecrate the community by doubling the material economy of the exchange of goods. This involves defining a homology between a plurality of spaces: the space between words that gathers them together on a page, the material space of their enunciation, the ideal space that their assemblage defines, the space in which humans come together to listen, look, and admire, and finally the ideal space that holds a community together. The fact is that Mallarmé spent much more time constructing the imaginary space of the séance and the Book than studying new rhythmic combinations. The question of rhythm is first of all, for him, the question that ties the forms of appearing—the unfolding and refolding of phenomena—to the form of communal "celebrations" to come.

RB & CG: You argue that in *Un coup de dés* Mallarmé extensively exploited the graphic dimension of writing to authenticate his intraliterary production of the Idea. He thereby secured the superiority of literature over music and ballet, fulfilling in a single stroke his poetic and political ambitions. However, you also show how Mallarmé ended up contradicting the antirepresentative ideal of his art: that is, in attempting to take advantage of the graphic possibilities of writing, he was led to produce a graphic representation of the movements of a ship and the upsurge of a Constellation. There is no doubt a certain bathos to this, given the antirepresentative ambitions Mallarmé had for his testamentary text. But is it truly possible to reduce the graphic dimensions of *Un coup de dés* to a mode of mimesis, and a rather banal one at that? What of the way its spatial disposition permits a multiplicity of syntactical and semantic combinations?

JR: It is a question of knowing what is meant by "antirepresentative." Mallarmé has antirepresentative ambitions inasmuch as he sets out to substitute combinations of words and rhythms, which are the *analoga* of the modes of unfolding of natural phenomena, for the mere description of the spectacles of nature. On this point, he is inscribed in the continuity of a problematic that traversed the entire Romantic epoch: that of expressing nature as a formative power instead of expressing it as the ensemble of constituted forms. And many of his poems are in fact constructed as movements of appearing, unfolding, and disappearing. The multiple syntactic and semantic combinations of which you speak are essentially constructed on this model of appearing, withdrawal, and dissimulation, lines that merge and move away from each other, symmetries and dissymmetries on the page. The "formal" side of these Mallarméan combinations respond to an essentially spatial model. The problem begins when the poem wants to show its material power of accomplishing the Idea by giving itself a space adequate to its statement. At this point, the process is inverted: the poem, which had gone from natural spectacles to the abstraction of forms of appearing, must take the opposite path in order to make its material presentation similar to what it says. No longer must the septuor of scintillations be evoked by words alone, it must be visualized on the page. Mallarmé is not the only writer in whose work antimimesis is transformed into hypermimesis. Think, for example, of the role played by the model of pantomime in reformers of dance and theatre like Noverre and Diderot in the eighteenth century. The "banality" of which you speak refers to the general problem of the language of performance: by setting aside representative models of narration and expression, this language tends towards a limit, which is that of the language of pantomime.

RB & CG: Returning to the question of your opposition to those for whom Mallarmé is an unequivocal elitist, it seems important to point out that your work nevertheless aims to clarify, rather than reject out of hand, the significance of the poet's subtraction from the public sphere. As you explain, the precariousness of Mallarmé's project to produce an authentic Idea determined that he had to denigrate other practices, such as music and ballet, and treat them as mere simulacra. To take another example, in your reading of "Conflict" you show how Mallarmé construes the drunken debauchery of the workers as a deficient expression of their aspiration towards emancipation—an aspiration that only the poet could properly fulfill. Despite, then, the implicit egalitarianism of his poetico-political project, might we say that it is the internal conflicts of literature itself—that is, of the literature of the aesthetic regime of art, which can only confirm its authenticity by exteriorizing its immanent fragility in other practices—which end up corrupting Mallarmé, turning him into an elitist? Might the case of Mallarmé show that the literary enterprise brings with it an inherent danger of elitist deviation?

JR: It is already significant that, in order to express his withdrawal, Mallarmé declares himself to be "on strike" with respect to society. And "Conflict" does not oppose the refinement of the elitist poet to the vulgarity of drunken workers. In his Sunday evening drunkenness, Mallarmé sees an expression of the desire for a beyond of the simple material economy. He discerns the most rudimentary expression of this need for a festive consecration of communal life, of which the poetic act represents the supreme form. This act of consecration is the privilege of the poet, but the poet himself is anybody, "whoever" [*quiconque veut*] (D 283). Any prosaic reality can give the material of this "anonymous magnificence" to the poem, which is tasked with succeeding the "Shadow of long ago" (D 247—*modified trans.*). And the privilege that Mallarmé gives to poetry with respect to other arts is not a privilege of elitist art over popular art. For him, poetry gives itself a more essential task than music or dance because it is an art of speech, an art capable of making the idea that animates it explicit. But it is to music and dance—and possibly to the dance of "music hall"—that he demands the means for renewing the language of poetry in order to render it adequate to this task. In any case, the notion of elitism is a far too simplistic way of posing the problem. Proust used to say, quite rightly, that so-called popular literature was more adapted to the tastes of the aristocrats of the Jockey Club than to the tastes of militant unionized workers. The convenient opposition of the elite and the popular in fact covers over a much more complex game of borrowings and appropriations. In the nineteenth century, literature takes up the new aspirations of the people in order to create a hitherto unknown tissue of sensations and a new scansion of novelistic time, while in order to think their condition, the emancipated workers take up the elevated feelings of romantic heroes.

The emancipation of the popular classes and the emancipation of literary speech intersect without becoming unified and echo each other without becoming identical.

RB & CG: Turning now to the relation of Mallarmé's politics to your own, there appears to be elements of his position that you yourself would explicitly affirm. For instance, Mallarmé's polemic against Wagner's recourse to a mythology of national origins, as well as his radical refusal of any identitarian incarnation for a human community, seem in principle to align with your own rejection of a politics based on preestablished identities. There also appears to be a similarity between Mallarmé's implicit opposition to the Saint-Simonian religion of labor and the emancipatory efforts of nineteenth-century workers, which you studied in *Proletarian Nights*. On the other hand, and as we mentioned above, you show that Mallarmé had to frame the worker in "Conflict" as incapable of emancipating himself without the guidance of the poet. How, then, would you describe the relationship of Mallarmé's politics to your own?

JR: There are certainly similarities between the two approaches, a same refusal of the grand mythologies of incarnation of the people of flesh and blood. That said, it is clear that my point of view is also that of a researcher who can confront, with the distance of a century, the elements of the Mallarméan project with those of German idealism, Romantic religions, workers' emancipation, or Wagnerian poetics. I can place the fictional encounter between the poet and the worker in "Conflict" or "Confrontation" in relation to that which effectively took place between workers and Saint-Simonian "priests" in the 1830s. The Saint-Simonian reference allows me to mark the tension that inhabits the Mallarméan poetic project. Mallarmé is critical with respect to the will of the "New Christianity," which so strongly marks the nineteenth century, and he is even more distant from all mythology of origins and roots. However, his vision of the poet's task as a sort of servant of a symbolic economy that remedies political economy is in the direct line of descent from his century's new "religions," which dream of a celebration of the sensible community that compensates for the formalism of the political community. In *Proletarian Nights,* I showed the gap between this project of the consecration of the community and the project of popular self-emancipation, most notably through the equivocations of the encounter between emancipated workers and Saint-Simonian priests.

RB & CG: Throughout the course of his posthumous reception, Mallarmé has frequently been mobilized as either a positive or a negative model for a politics of literature. Whether construed as a counter-revolutionary nihilist or a progressive, he has allowed such diverse thinkers as Jean-Paul Sartre, the Telquellians, and Jean-Claude Milner to define their own political positions—positions that involved either a rupture with, or a fidelity to, Mallarmé. Your work, however, seems to break with this interpretative tendency. For instead of strategically constituting Mallarmé as a model to emulate or expiate, you pursue a more recognizably philological project, which seeks to restore his writings to their proper horizon of significance and to map as precisely as possible the tensions in them between egalitarianism and elitism. Could we nevertheless say that there is a strategic side to your work? You often speak of restoring past practices to their proper horizon of significance in order to intervene into the present moment. Could your work on Mallarmé therefore be seen as a kind of strategic intervention, one which takes a paradoxically philological path?

JR: First of all, let us say that I was not concerned to mark a tension between egalitarianism and elitism in Mallarmé. I was concerned with rethinking the role that he attributes to poetry and to the meaning of his poetic inventions. This supposed a divergence from the dominant *doxa*, which made Mallarmé a hero of the modernist rupture and rendered equivalent his poetic revolution and Marxist revolution in the name of an equivalence between historical materialism and the poetic primacy of the signifier. In my work, the "philological" project has two sides to it. On the one hand, it is a matter of recreating the universe of the circulation of words, significations, tonalities, and affects at the heart of which a singular speech makes itself heard, instead of measuring this speech against a norm that has been dogmatically posited between the old and the new, the progressive and the reactionary, etc. But, on the other hand, it is also a matter of expanding this singular circulation by showing how the conditions of production and reception of a poetic speech greatly exceed the literary field; that they sketch out a scene of speech that can be placed in relation with other scenes of speech that belong to an apparently very different universe, from the rules of religious asceticism to the formulations of political conflict, to those of social emancipation. There is no contradiction between philological precision and strategic intervention. It is necessary to be very precise "philologically" in order to understand the forms and stakes of a scene of speech and to understand in the same stroke how they redistribute, in broader terms, the givens of a distribution of the sensible. Thinking this relation between a historically situated scene of speech and a symbolic distribution of possible speech, whose forms and effects traverse the ages, leads at the same time to an overturning of the relations between the present and the past, and the relations between the universal and the particular. This allows us to call on, in a particular present, other blocs of the present. We can thus destabilize the regime of the perceptible and the thinkable that founds the order of societies. We can put into question the established relations between the order of times and the links between causes and effects, which found the false evidences of thought. Reading the speech of Saint-Simonian workers from the 1830s led me to put into question, bit by bit, all of the false evidences of the history of modern revolutions and their destiny. Confronting the speech of Mallarmé with those of the poets who effectively inspired him, but also confronting his thought of writing with that of the pedagogues of the Republic, his poetic project with the ceremonies of the Saint-Simonian religion, or his thought of "types" with that of modernist designers, allowed me to shatter the false evidences of modernist dogmas and to rethink the history of the adventures of modern art and of its relation to the order and disorder of societies.

INFLUENCES AND INTERLOCUTORS

RB & CG: Among the works of Mallarmé scholarship that you draw on, it seems as though Bertrand Marchal's *La Religion de Mallarmé* played a role in forming your own reading. It is perhaps unsurprising that you would be receptive to Marchal's book, since it was one of the first systematic explorations of the spiritual and utopian dimensions of Mallarmé's writings as they are developed in *Divagations*. Marchal's study of the sociopolitical and spiritual aspects of Mallarmé's vision proves how the most formally inventive of poets can simultaneously show an exemplary concern for social and political matters—an apparent paradox that your own framework of the aesthetic regime of art accounts for. How would you describe your relationship to Marchal's work? More specifically, where Marchal speaks of religion, you speak of politics, thereby appearing to break at this precise point with his resolutely philological approach. What is at stake for you in this shift?

JR: I was certainly pleased to find in Bertrand Marchal's book a radical divergence with respect to the habitual readings of Mallarmé in terms of pure poetry, autotelism or the primacy of the signifier, and an attention to the "religious" preoccupations that undergird Mallarmé's "formal inventions," which inscribe him in his time and motivate his poetic researches. For me, it is the best book ever written on Mallarmé. For all that, I would not say that it played a formative role in my own reading. The latter is in effect largely determined by all of my work on the nineteenth century and on the obsessions that not only traversed it but properly constituted it: the first of these obsessions is that of a "new religion," which means two things: a terrestrial and human religion as opposed to the religions of divine transcendence, but also a new form of the sensible link between men that goes beyond the limits of the political community. This obsession marks, notably, the "New Christianity" of Saint-Simonism, the religiosity of the 1848 Revolution, the multiplicity of utopian religions or the attempts to create a civil republican religion. It also marks, in a very diverse manner, the Hölderlian dream of the new aesthetic church, the Wagnerian resurrection of old Germanic divinities, Hugolian pantheism, the Rimbauldian dream of a truth possessed in a body and in a soul, etc. For me, the "politics of the siren" is to be thought of in this context. It is not a politics in the strict sense of the term. It is one of the numerous attempts to supplement or replace politics by a "religious" link. I proposed the term metapolitics to think the ensemble of these attempts. If I nevertheless use the term "politics," it is in order to mark the following tension: it is not only a matter of religion but of "religion" such as the Romantic age thinks it, that is, as a supplement or a substitute for the reign of governments and laws.

RB & CG: One of the most striking aspects of your work on Mallarmé is the insistence on the centrality of a certain form of mimesis in his literary project. Indeed, you directly dispute Derrida's well-known interpretation of the poet, which involved the claim that Mallarmé undercut the primacy of the Platonic model of mimesis and inscribed it within a more expansive logic. Against this deconstructive reading, you assert that Mallarmé aimed to imitate an authentic Idea in his poetry—an Idea that corresponded to the human community in its chimerical essence. Your disagreement with Derrida on this point rests on your attentiveness to the immanent principles of Mallarmé's project: that is, you are explicitly concerned with how he himself conceived of this task, and seek to accurately reconstitute its logic. Thus while Derrida may indeed have demonstrated that Mallarmé deconstructed the Platonic model of mimesis, you show that the logic of his project required him to rigorously and self-consciously maintain an essentialist form of mimesis. How do you understand the balance between what Mallarmé may be seen to have effectively achieved in his work, even if unconsciously, and what he self-consciously set out to do? If your aim is to restore his project to its proper horizon of significance, could this come at the cost of missing a more radical logic in Mallarmé's work, such as the one Derrida identifies? Do you risk turning his project into a simple historical curiosity?

JR: I have always been interested, on the one hand, in what people wanted to do, and on the other, in what they did do, and in the possible difference between the two. But I have always been suspicious of approaches that are attached to showing what people were doing without wanting to. As for Derrida's analysis, I think that it teaches us more about his project than about Mallarmé's. Derrida must do violence to Mallarmé's text in order to make it the "pure medium of fiction," a virgin surface, a pure spacing that precedes all inscription (D 140). This torsion prolongs Mallarmé's own artifice, which already feigned to forget that the gestures of Paul Marguerite followed the text of a very detailed written monologue. Derrida in turn wants to see Mallarmé's text as a critique of the Platonic model of the primacy of the imitated over the imitator. But the fact that the mimicry illustrates the idea, and not an effective action, does not cancel out the fact that it illustrates it perfectly well. The "yet unwritten page" is, in fact, as in Plato, a prewritten page (D 140). But at the time of *Tel Quel* Mallarmé had to appear as the champion of the deconstruction of logocentrism, to the point that it was necessary for a character of radical novelty to be given to analyses and expressions that Mallarmé actually takes from Gautier and Banville. That said, the root of the problem for me is to be found elsewhere: the concept of mimesis, in the context of which the novelty of literature can be thought, is not simply the concept of the resemblance between thought and its inscription. It is the concept of a legislation of resemblances that itself belongs to a global distribution of the sensible. The concept of mimesis is to be thought in the context of an entire system of relations between the high and the low, seeing and knowing, seeing and doing—a system that also defines an entire distribution of positions and capacities whose centerpiece is the famous Platonic impossibility of doing two things at once. In Mallarmé, mimesis is at work on a much broader terrain than that which is circumscribed in the little text commented on by Derrida. It is at play in the substitution of types and "aspects" for images. This substitution implies a thought of appearance that does not confront it with being. And it is in play at another level in the thought of a symbolic economy that doubles the real economy as another system of signs. It is in the relation between these two levels that Mallarméan mimesis and its relation with the Plato of the *Laws*—who is perhaps more important than the Plato of the *Philebus*—can be thought.

RB & CG: In an interview given after the publication of *The Politics of the Siren*, you stated that your interpretation of Mallarmé was produced in dialogue with the work of Alain Badiou.[1] In fact, Badiou would seem to be one of your most important contemporary interlocutors when it comes to the philosophical significance of Mallarmé. What is so important about the way Badiou reads Mallarmé for you?

JR: I do not recall that interview. In the book itself, I indicated that I took Alain Badiou's interpretation of a poem into account, but I was not concerned to confirm or refute it. In fact, I did not write the book to criticize Badiou's reading of Mallarmé. It was rather the opposite: I used his reading of Mallarmé when, later on, I had to speak of Badiou's thought, notably with respect to its relation to art. I then used it as an example that allowed me to characterize Badiou's method—and, perhaps, to oppose it to my own. But at the outset the question of reading Mallarmé was for me included in a much broader opposition. I firstly criticized the representation of Mallarmé as a hero of modernism, and of modernism as the exploration of the medium and the means specific to an artistic practice. If this representation is not proper to Badiou, he shares it, and his "subtractive" conception of Mallarméan poetry is consistent with the dominant representation that identifies the modern artistic revolution with an abstraction of represented content. This vision is clearly opposed to my own, for which the destruction of the mimetic order is not a destruction of representation but of the system of divisions and hierarchies in the context of which the mimetic order functions. Badiou takes up the traditional conception of the specificity of disciplines and ties it to his idea of a separation of truth procedures. On the one hand, then, he is consistent with the dominant vision of modernist "abstraction," but on the other hand his "Platonism" makes him confer a purely ethical function on poetry and this translates into his practice of reading poets—a practice similar to the gnomic reading Adorno detects in Heidegger. He finds maxims and lessons there. Ultimately, he uses these to illustrate philosophical theses. On the contrary, I endeavored to place Mallarmé's poetic project back into the context of the politico-religious programs of his century and to show that he responds to them not by philosophical statements but by singular performances, that is, by effective performances in which the poem is structured in the form of a fan that unfolds and refolds, or by dreamed-of performances such as the project of the Book and its séances.

RB & CG: In your reading of Badiou, you argue that he places philosophy above poetry by virtue of its capacity to pronounce on its truth—a truth of which poetry is itself unaware.[2] Against this hierarchization, you praise the dialectical procedure of *Theory of the Subject* and make the striking claim that Badiou's own distribution and hierarchization of discourses is built upon a prior moment at which they are indistinct, or rather radically equal. Put differently, you claim that he effectively treats philosophy and poetry as equally capable of thought, but that he nevertheless disavows this in his post-*Being and Event* work. Could we construe your preference for Badiou's procedure in *Theory of the Subject* as an implicit directive for contemporary readings of Mallarmé? That is, should philosophical interpretations of Mallarmé begin with the axiom that there exists a fundamental equality between the capacity of poetry and philosophy to think?

JR: It is not a matter of personal preference. I marked the difference between the places Mallarmé occupies in the successive analyses Badiou devoted to him. There is a moment where for him Mallarmé plays the role of the thinker of the event who provides philosophy itself with a model of rationality. This is the case in *Being and Event*. And then there is a moment, from *Conditions* onwards, where he plays the specific role of the poet who produces a truth of which he is unaware and which philosophy must decipher. If we consider the first moment, we observe that the different forms of rationality are not separated and hierarchized, and that they communicate between themselves according to procedures of condensation arising from a general poetics (think of the way in which the notion of "site" makes mathematics communicate with poetry). My argument is not that poetry and philosophy are equal.

It is that there exists a level of thought at which their very distinction does not exist—a level at which operations of thought take place that do not belong to any particular category and which testify to something common in thought and language, something that belongs to all. This does not mean I am unaware of their specificities. There are certainly types of operations of thought and language that are different. What seems problematic to me is to relate them to specific disciplines and competencies, and to posit a form of thought whose vocation is to pronounce on the thought contained in the others. From this point of view, Badiou is a faithful disciple of Althusser, for whom theory must reveal the truth of practices, practices that know not what they do. It is here that, for me, we find the fundamental choice defining the opposition between equality and inequality: either we speak from a privileged position that distributes roles and examines how each person is carrying out theirs, or we speak from a common level of thought.

RB & CG: In striking contrast to both your own and Badiou's reading of Mallarmé, in *Mallarmé au tombeau* Jean-Claude Milner sees Mallarmé as a strictly counterrevolutionary figure, whose reactionary nihilism led him to deny the reality of political events such as the abortive Revolution of 1848. In Milner's terms, we must break with Mallarmé if we are to properly think the nineteenth and twentieth centuries—and therefore leave him to rest in his *tombeau*. Can your utopian reading of Mallarmé resist the forceful conviction of Milner's image of the poet?

JR: Milner wants first and foremost to make Mallarmé the poet who buried the nineteenth century and its revolutionary ideals in the tomb. To do this, he too has to use a *symptomal* method and to find with all his might—in a poem by Mallarmé that speaks of an imprisoned swan—an assessment of the defeated Revolution of 1848. He must above all render eternal what Mallarmé refers to as the absence of a present. He wants to make Mallarmé the tomb of all of the futures dreamed of by the nineteenth century. For him, Mallarmé is the poet who says: "The century did not take place, it cannot be added to." It is clear that Mallarmé's writings run counter to such an enterprise. For him, the century took place and there is something to be added to it, namely, a new way of accomplishing what it was seeking. Certainly, Mallarmé never shared any revolutionary aspirations. This is also why he did not need to produce an assessment of them and declare them over. On the contrary, he shared many of the aspirations that marked his century, notably, the project of a new terrestrial religion and a new poetry that would prepare the "celebrations of the future." Far from bringing the ideals of the Romantic century to a close, he makes them communicate with those of the avant-garde of the technological century by proposing a new formula that disincarnates the religion of the community and renders the "intoxication of art" susceptible to coinciding with an "industrial accomplishment" (D 135).

RB & CG: In the final chapter of *The Politics of the Siren*, you attempt to demonstrate why Mallarmé's project had to fail. The first reason for this is the contingent relation of content and form that inheres in the aesthetic regime of art. The second is the exacerbation of this contingency in literary modernity by the problematic of *orphaned speech*, which is your term for the capacity of the written word to be taken up by anyone and made to mean anything. Strictly speaking, then, Mallarmé's project to institute a new Eucharist had to fail, or rather be eternally deferred, for it always risked turning into a dead letter. However, in his recent work *The Number and the Siren* (2011), Quentin Meillassoux argues that *Un coup de dés* did indeed succeed. For the real sacrificial drama of the poem to take place, Meillassoux thinks, the discovery of the code could not be guaranteed in advance but rather had to rely on the anarchic logic of reception implied by *orphaned speech*. In other words, rather than determining literature's inability to live up to its Idea, this logic is actually the condition of possibility for Mallarmé's success. Could Meillassoux's arguments force a reconsideration of your own reading of *Un coup de dés?* Might this last great work of Mallarmé's be the sole text to have transcended the contradictions of the aesthetic regime of art?

JR: I have not yet had the chance to read Quentin Meillassoux's book. I will content myself with clarifying the question of "success" and "failure." I situated Mallarmé's work in the context of a tension between the free circulation of the orphaned letter and the inverse project whose nostalgia it provokes: the entirely motivated letter, the incarnate word, the truth inscribed in the flesh of things. The project that defines literature as a particular historical figure is that of producing a new form of incarnation on the very basis of the solitude of the orphaned letter. If we judge it in the strategic terms of the adaptation of means to ends, we will of course say that this project is doomed to fail, and we will seek the formula that transcends its contradiction, or we will find in these contradictions the prophecy of its imminent death, and the emergence of a new figure. It is precisely this strategic conception that I have always objected to. The contradictions of a regime are not what limits it or dooms it to disappearance. They are, on the contrary, what give it life and its own dynamism. I once said that many more possibilities were always engendered by an unrealizable project than by a realizable one. The contradictions of literature are at the source of the multiple riches of its inventions. And the richest of these inventions are not those of writers who think they have found the formula, the code, or the figure in the carpet. These riches are those of writers who have measured themselves up to the impossibility of their dream: hybrid works like *In Search of Lost Time*, incomplete or unachievable works like *Bouvard and Pécuchet*, *Finnegans Wake* or *The Man Without Qualities*... It is possible that in *Un coup de dés*, Mallarmé found and realized the formula. But our interest in the work then remains measured by what the poet wanted to do more than by what he did. And what is then called "success" consists in the fact of having effected a narrowing of the field of possibilities or impossibilities. This kind of success interests me very little. What interests me is the way in which failure itself—the impossibility of realizing his project—defines a success, a singular invention of language and thought. It is to hold two apparently contradictory propositions together: that of Proust—"At the Last judgment of works intentions do not count"—and that of Rilke—"Losing too is still ours."

NOTES

1. "Mallarmé, un poète infiniment attentif à son temps: entretien avec Jacques Rancière," *La Lettre horlieu -(X)*, No. 5, 1997, pp. 23–39.
2. Jacques Rancière, "The Poet at the Philosopher's: Mallarmé and Badiou" in PL 183–204.

Chapter Two

"I Believed I Owed Mallarmé the Truth"

Jean-Claude Milner

STRUCTURALISM, LINGUISTICS, SCIENCE

Robert Boncardo & Christian R. Gelder: The period of your intellectual formation—namely, your involvement in the *Cahiers pour l'analyse*—was contemporaneous with the explosion of structuralism as an intellectual paradigm. As a minor chapter in this adventure of thought, there was an intensification of interest in Mallarmé, who was understood as both a theoretician and practitioner of the signifier. Derrida's "The Double Session," for instance, as well as various articles in the journals *Tel Quel* and *Change*, attest to this. What role, if any, did Mallarmé play at this time in your intellectual career? Was he an important point of reference for those around you?

Jean-Claude Milner: Unlike you, I do not believe that structuralism rekindled an interest in Mallarmé. Barthes, for example, did not make a significant intervention. Foucault's few paragraphs in *The Order of Things* are profound, but remain programmatic. Lacan practiced the art of the sonnet at the school of Mallarmé, but allowed nothing to be published. As for Derrida, today I accord him great importance but precisely for contrary reasons. Note the date: 1969. May 1968 marked the end of the structuralist movement in the strict sense because this movement was tied to the quasi-disappearance of the political engagement of intellectuals, from the end of the Algerian War. Engagement is reborn after '68, even if it is not in its Sartrean form. In my view, post-68 modernity is antistructuralist. Derrida attests to this, especially as several of his interventions are directed against the great figures of structuralism: Saussure, Lévi-Strauss, Foucault, and Lacan. "The Double Session" is inscribed in this project.

To come back to what concerns me more particularly, I did not frequent the doctrinal writings of Mallarmé; for me, he counted as a poet, but I was not passionate about him. Structuralism did not engage with him. At the time, Baudelaire's prose and poetry was much more captivating. I worked with Jakobson on a reading of *Spleen IV* in terms of anagrams; at the time, an anagrammatic approach did not seem fruitful for Mallarmé. I think precisely the opposite today: anagrams are fundamental for him. But no matter. While Baudelaire never left me, I came to Mallarmé very late.

RB & CG: Many French philosophers and linguists have drawn on Mallarmé when elucidating their own theses on language. In *Les noms indistincts*, you propose a powerful and moving reading of the final and famous section of *Un coup de dés*. As you argue, the upsurge of the Constellation at the end of the poem stages a brief, scintillating encounter between the three orders of language: the Real, the Symbolic, and the Imaginary. Although more than thirty years have passed since the publication of *Les noms indistincts* do you still see the possibility of a mutually illuminating conversation between Lacan and Mallarmé, as if both were singular stars in the constellation of modern thought on language?

JCM: Mallarmé mattered to Lacan: not only the poetry, but also the Book. The notes deciphered by Jacques Scherer offer a glimpse of an organisation, from which Lacan took inspiration when he founded *la Cause freudienne*. The dialogue of the dead is a genre no longer practiced much anymore—it would take a great mind to write the one you mention. I would like to think that it would initially focus on this collective organisation and on the relationship it maintains with the following decisive questions: does language unite or separate speaking beings? Is it the place of their simultaneous presence or their alternating absence? Does the Book not announce the analytic session, where a speaking being listens to another speaking being say the text of their subjectivization? Then, the dialogue would focus on language: must we distinguish language [*la langue*] from Language [*le langage*]? Does language [*la langue*] reveal or obscure Language [*le langage*]? The modern reflection on language begins, it seems to me, with the following affirmation that we read in Meillet, who was a direct student of Saussure: the name *bird* does not designate the bird that is there, but the one who has taken flight. The signified consists in the absence of the signified thing. How can we not link these aphorisms to Mallarmé's flower, which is "absent from every bouquet" (D 210)? Is this the same absence? If yes, then the condition of possibility of language as an object of a Galilean science, and the condition of possibility of language as a poetic material, are one and the same. I claim that the Lacanian notion of the *signifier* sums up this unicity. Finally, the question of chance would arise. Mallarmé accuses Victor Hugo of having annexed "whoever tried to think, discourse, and narrate" to verse (D 202). It is with this that he wants to break. We are therefore permitted to reconstruct his doctrine via the systematic inversion of Hugo: *verse does not think, does not discourse, and does not narrate*. On this secret condition, verse can accomplish the effect that Mallarmé himself explicitly assigns to it: to abolish chance—the chance, notably, that structures the encounter between sound and sense. In other words, verse does not think, nor does it discourse, nor narrate; it abolishes chance. This formula recalls Freud's own: the dream does not think, nor calculate, nor judge; it transforms. Lacan comments on Freud and extends his formula to the unconscious itself: the unconscious does not think, nor calculate, nor judge; it works. What is the relationship between the dreamwork and the work of verse? In both cases, it is a matter of the signifier: the encryption of the dream and the play of sounds in verse. What is the relation between the work of the unconscious and the work of verse? In both cases, is it a matter of the abolition of chance. It is remarkable that the parapraxis and the slip embodies, *par excellence*, the grip that chance has on the speaking being. With the name unconscious, Freud showed the necessity that governs them. More broadly, we can consider that the entirety of psychoanalysis undertakes to abolish chance, not in the name of poetry, certainly, but in the name of science. Lacan takes all of this up; in some way he associates Freud and Mallarmé under the heading of the signifier. But in doing so, he uncovers the equivocity of chance. I think that he would have interrogated Mallarmé on this point. He would have asked him why chance ends up resembling necessity. But, then, what does the abolition of chance produce? The Real?

RB & CG: In your essay "The Tell-Tale Constellations," you address the question of how nineteenth-century poets confronted the mathematization of Nature in post-Galilean science. For you, modern science demonstrates that phenomenal experience is no longer the measure of all things. By virtue of its mathematization, a distant and unobservable planet could be granted a greater degree of reality than a constellation. While a constellation might appear before our eyes, invested with cosmological and ideological significance, for modern science it remains irreducibly imaginary. You argue that Mallarmé was exemplarily conscious of these issues. However, you also recognize in his *œuvre* the presence of motifs related to the cycles of nature, the solar drama and, more generally, the tradition of the *liber mundi*. How, then, do you understand the relation between the universe of post-Galilean science and the way these more traditional cosmological images operate in Mallarmé?

JCM: Mallarmé wanted, I believe, to bring mathematization and literalization as close together as possible. He was a reader and translator of Poe, who wrote *Eureka* as well as a treatise on poetic composition. The tradition of the *liber mundi*, the rules of the alexandrine, their relation to the zodiac and the seven stars of the Great Bear are *allusions* to the calculability of the universe; when I say allusions, I mean it. They are not the laws of calculation themselves. These allusions do not deny calculation, but remain exterior to it. The constellation is imaginary insofar as it is seen, but it alludes to the stars, which are real as they are neither seen nor imagined except by hyperbole. I refer here to the first word of "Prose (pour des Esseintes)." From the numerations and the rhythms of the finite world, we pass by way of hyperbole to the mathematical laws of the modern universe. I refer you to the qualifier *hyperscientific* that Mallarmé uses to describe modernity. Hyperbole thus breaches the limit, but under the following conditions: (a) that it begins from the world, in opposition to the universe; (b) that this opposition annuls itself as soon as hyperbole rejoins the universe; (c) that the Book guarantees, by its own calculations, that the limit be breached.

If the third condition (c) is met, then in the aphorism "everything in the world exists to end up as a book" (D 226), the phrase "everything in the world" is strictly the translation of the term *universe*. If the Book existed, it would not contradict Galilean science, it would accomplish it.

But if, as I believe, it turns out in the end that the third condition (c) is not met, then it is necessary to understand the following: that the world is imaginary, only the universe is real, the universe exists for nothing, a poem can at most let the murmur of this nothing be heard. The *Coup de dés* certainly ends on a hyperbole, but this latter does not produce any junction between a book and the universe; it rather recalls a Möbius strip where the recto continues on the verso: "as far as place can fuse with the beyond [...] A CONSTELLATION" (CP 114). We cannot transcend the constellation, not even by allusion.

RB & CG: Continuing with "The Tell-Tale Constellations," you end this essay by distinguishing between mathematized science and mathematics. Specifically, you say that Mallarmé made mathematics an ally in his quest to inscribe a poetic exception to the universe of post-Galilean science. How do you see the relationship between mathematics and verse in Mallarmé in particular, and in modern poetry more generally?

JCM: I have partially responded to your question. The calculations of verse are mathematical. The same goes for the calculations that we glimpse in the Book. These calculations are, it seems to me, very simple: they boil down to addition and, in the case of the Book, multiplication. But, as simple as they are, they are mathematical.

I wish commentators were more attentive to this point. If, with respect to Gödel, we can speak of the arithmetization of logic, it is not only because he assigned a number to diverse logical entities (operators, variables, etc.)—a number that cannot be another once it is assigned—it is above all because he defined these numbers by arithmetical operations, essentially multiplication and factorial decomposition. It is the same with Mallarmé. The seven of the dice is mathematical only because it is attained thanks to addition—or, more precisely, thanks to a nontrivial property of addition, namely, commutativity: $1 + 6 = 6 + 1 = 2 + 5 = 5 + 2 = 3 + 4$, etc. By itself, the seven of the Great Bear is not mathematical, insofar as it is limited to the "septuor," but it becomes so when related to other sevens, such as the seven of the dice or the seven of the name *Anatole*. Only then can we sever seven from what it counts (septuor) or does not count (dice). It becomes mathematical *a fortiori* when it is obtained by adding $4 + 3$, as it happens in the sonnet: a quatrain plus a tercet. The twelve of the alexandrine and the fourteen of the sonnet are based on associativity. It seems that in the Book multiplication plays a central role.

It seems to me that Quentin Meillassoux neglected this point. In his commentary on the *Coup de dés*, I would say that no mathematical property of addition is implemented. The number 707, to which he is lead, is the result of a sum of the type $1 + 1 + 1...$, with neither commutativity nor associativity. Moreover, this number is such that we cannot and must not engage in any operation on it. Rather, it lends itself to a verbal game, "seven without seven," *sept sans sept*, which, in my eyes, refers to Mallarmé's abandonment of all his previous ambitions for verse. In any case, the calculative ambition of the Book is abandoned. If Meillassoux is right in his counting, then he has shown the opposite of what he wanted: Mallarmé renounced the Book.

MALLARMÉ, POLITICS, HISTORY

RB & CG: Perhaps now we can turn to your most sustained reading of the poet, which first appeared under the title *Mallarmé au tombeau* in 1999, and was republished, alongside *Constat* and *Le Triple de Plaisir*, in 2002.[1] In the first half of this book, you offer a meticulous reading of the relation between Mallarmé, Hugo, and Baudelaire by examining the sonnet "Le vierge, le vivace et le bel aujourd'hui." In the second half, however, the tone of the book changes to one of polemic, whereby you charge the twentieth-century's "strict Mallarméans" (MT 88) with having carried out the doctrine of political nihilism you discern, provocatively, in Mallarmé. What motivated you to intervene into the domain of Mallarmé studies at this point of your intellectual trajectory? Outside of this domain, what broader context were you hoping to address via this striking reading, especially given that at the close of the book you essentially ask readers to leave the poet to rest in his tomb?

JCM: Just like many of my contemporaries after May '68, the question of politics, which is linked to the question of revolution, occupied me in the form of leftist radicalism. Around 1973, I ceased to be a Maoist but from this engagement I retained a great mistrust of the parliamentary left. This left's return to power in 1981, after more than twenty years, and then the fall of the Berlin wall and its aftermath in 1989 punctuated my interest in politics. I think of politics as distinct from both its parliamentary and its radical version. In fact, I only admit a minimalist version of politics: that politics is nothing more and nothing less than a procedure allowing us to treat the multiplicity of speaking bodies. How can we ensure that bodies do not cease to be speaking bodies when they are gathered together? Moreover, the question of linguistics as a science has also occupied me since the mid-60s. After the Maoist years were put on hold, this question led me to frequent Mitsou Ronat, who was to closely study the *Coup de dés*, and Jacques Roubaud, a poet and mathematician, who published important discoveries regarding Mallarmé's sonnets. With François Regnault, I wrote a treatise on the diction of the alexandrine by drawing on linguistics. In short, linguistics led me to poetics, poetics brought me back to politics, and then politics led me to prose. Indeed, during this period, I not only renewed ties for a time with Alain Badiou, whose work you know, but I also met Natacha Michel who, as a novelist, was working on prose and its relation to politics: is there politics only in prose? If so, what should prose be? And what becomes of poetry? The sonnet of the Swan seemed to me to tie together all these threads. Only then did it occur to me that all these questions touching on the survival of speaking bodies, the persistence of speech, prose, poetry, modern science, and technology were knotted together in a single question: the rupture that constitutes the destruction of the European Jews.

Many of my contemporaries had only one concern: forgetting the ruptures that the history of the twentieth century left us. Whenever politics made them despair, they found hope in poetry; if poetry disappointed them, they turned towards some fragment of political consolation; if these fragments decidedly did not suffice, they turned to metaphysics. One would think it a game—and in this game, Mallarmé seemed to offer a winning combination, since without having to leave him behind one found in him every possible loophole. First you lent Mallarmé your own illusions, then you claimed he agreed with you. Rancière, a hasty reader, found there the justification for his blind trust in the left of 1981; others who were more careful found a radical politics that was dear to them. For my part, I believed I owed Mallarmé the truth; besides, he preceded me in concluding that restricted action had become a caricature of itself; it had failed just as much as Hugo's expansive action; what was important led to an impasse; we emerged from the impasse only by abandoning what was most important. In my eyes, it was to pay tribute to him to wrest him away from the follies of his faithful.

RB & CG: *Mallarmé au tombeau* culminates in a stunning reading of the constellation in *Un coup de dés*. You take this seminal moment as emblematic of Mallarmé's overall doctrine: that poetry, figured as the Constellation, exists at an infinite distance from the world—a world that the poet condemns as the site of a mere scattering of insignificant events. While this moment is the climax of *Mallarmé au tombeau*, you have nevertheless proposed a number of other, perhaps mutually exclusive, interpretations of this image. Leaving aside *Les noms indistincts*, do you see a relation between, on the one hand, the constellation as you read it in "The Tell-Tale Constellations," and on the other hand as it emerges in a seemingly distinct sense in *Mallarmé au tombeau*? If your first reading relates to science and the second to politics, might there be a relationship between post-Galilean science and political nihilism?

JCM: I recognize that my reading of Mallarmé's politics has evolved. Initially I thought I had deciphered a revolutionary purism in him: the clatter of dice, the smoke of a cigar, the beat of a fan seemed to me to be allegories of the real revolution, detached from all of the mediocre examples proposed by the various revolutionary movements. I speak of a *real* revolution, as opposed to imaginary revolutions: 1848 or the Commune. Subsequently, I concluded that in fact there was no real revolution for Mallarmé beyond imaginary revolutions. This is how I read "Le vierge, le vivace et le bel aujourd'hui," or how I interpreted the fleetingly heard phrase "the penultimate is dead" in "The Demon of Analogy." This is not Mallarmé's evolution, but an evolution in my reading of him. That being said, my first reading and my second have a common point of departure: Mallarmé's contempt for imaginary revolutions—a contempt taken from Baudelaire, in opposition to Hugo. One thing seems certain to me: in both the first and second readings, this contempt leads Mallarmé to reject the Third Republic insofar as it combines two dishonorable traits: (a) it presents itself as the heir to what is imaginary in revolutions; (b) it betrays this imaginary. This is not to say that Mallarmé did not consider the republic preferable to other forms of government. But if he preferred it, it is precisely because it does not claim to go beyond *l'inférieur clapotis quelconque*.[2] It is intrinsically linked to the prose of universal reportage, to the Newspaper as opposed to Literature. Those who claim to identify an attempt at a civil religion in the Book, inscribed in the ideal operation of the republic, are completely mistaken. If it were to exist, the Book would on the contrary enable an escape from the republic and reportage, which are united in what Mallarmé calls the Newspaper.

We can see here a reflection of my personal attitude towards the French and global political reality. With the left's coming to power in 1981, I recognized the double movement of 1875: to pose as the heir to what is imaginary in past revolutions, to seize upon this so as to betray it all the better. More generally, the fall of the statues of Lenin and the disaster of the Cultural Revolution led me to conclude that the Russian and Chinese revolutions were imaginary. That said, I do not conclude that the real revolution was necessarily a phantasm. In this, I am closer to Baudelaire than to Mallarmé.

You mention science—you are right to. It took a long time for people to understand that Galilean science, integrally mathematized and/or literalized, is radically indifferent to politics. Political indifference can lead to political nihilism. But in Mallarmé's case, political nihilism does not come to him from science; on the contrary, it comes from his failure to construct a positive form of gathering that excepts itself from the Crowd.

RB & CG: Turning to the question of the Book, in the final chapter of *Mallarmé au tombeau* you write that Mallarmé failed "to establish the Book as an institution of reading and perpetual diction" (MT 78). For you, Mallarmé's rejection of the role of spiritual guide—of the poetic purveyor of utopianism, a role played exemplarily by Hugo before him—is encapsulated in the failure of the Book and then given expression in the cold poetic nihilism of *Un coup de dés*. In "The Tell-Tale Constellations," you also draw a link between the failure of the Book and *Un coup de dés*, arguing that Mallarmé began by believing that "everything in the world exists to end up as a book"—in the sense that the world was properly the domain of poetry, rather than of post-Galilean science—but that he stopped believing this in 1897 with the publication of *Un coup de dés*. Given that you present a resolutely nihilist Mallarmé, how do you understand the communitarian and utopian project of the Book? Could you explain the relationship you posit between the failure of the Book, Mallarmé's nihilism, and his acceptance of post-Galilean science?

JCM: First of all, Mallarmé has a positive reading of allegory. I note that I take this term from Baudelaire: "everything for me becomes allegory"[3] echoes "everything in the world exists to end up as a book" (D

226). Verse authorizes the allegorical passage from the constellation, as a visible image, to invisible celestial bodies. The Book was supposed to publicly legitimize this passage. Then, the Book having failed, the reading becomes more restrictive: allegory is not a promise of passage but a nonpassage, an external limit to Galilean calculation. "Nature has taken place; it can't be added to" (D 187). This maxim ends up taking on a nihilist sense: we can't add a Book to nature, we can't add action, and we can't add politics. I think this hypothesis was made explicit much earlier than claimed; the sonnet of the Swan is already marked by it. I am not saying that it prevailed from the outset. I admit that Mallarmé swayed over several decades but he swayed in a proper sense: certain texts go in one direction, while others in the opposite. Sometimes within the same text we perceive a fluctuation. But the nihilist hypothesis wins out in the end. In my view, *Un coup de dés* is the final expression of this hypothesis.

"It can't be added to" can be interpreted as "it can be subtracted from." The Book appeared more and more as an addition. The *Coup de dés* concludes with a final displacement: having abandoned the Book, Mallarmé refocuses on subtraction and exception; the word *except* functions as a pivot for the text. By this, it reverses all his previous work in the direction of subtraction and saves it from what appears now as a perverse temptation: the Book, far from subtracting, adds—and what does it add? The worst: a mixture of collectivity and cult. Some have recognized in it the shadow of a religion without God. If they are right, it must be added that, precisely for this reason, Mallarmé turned away from it in disgust.

In this final moment, he no longer hopes for anything from a collective form. Insufficient emphasis has been placed on the decadence of the *Mardis*; as literary and worldly curiosity about Mallarmé grew around him, they became a veritable carnival. The visitor's descriptions (notably those of the English) leave no room for doubt. This is why I said that restricted action had become a caricature of itself. Likewise, we cannot stress enough Mallarmé's growing indifference to Wagner and Bayreuth. In the preface to the *Coup de dés*, he insists on music but never mentions the opera. He speaks of the symphony. He also speaks of concerts. But is the concert something other than a crowd determined by chance? This is doubtful. If no collective form can resist the attraction of the phenomenon of the crowd (for example: the *Mardis* and concerts), then no utopia is of value since all utopias begin with a conjecture on collective forms.

But this conclusion is drawn only at the very end of his trajectory. Mallarmé began by thinking that poetry could become an organiser, not by making itself the echo of overtly political gatherings (this was Hugo's final choice, who becomes the poetic companion of republicanism), but on the contrary by separating itself from them. The hypothesis of the Book affirms that from poetry a collectivity will arise, from its diction, from the perpetuation of this diction. If I dared, I would say that what the Book is for Mallarmé is analogous to what the Party is for Lenin. The failure is obvious in both cases but unlike Lenin, Mallarmé realized it.

RB & CG: At the close of *Mallarmé au tombeau*, you draw a series of suggestive links between Mallarmé's political nihilism and his two literary successors, Paul Valéry and André Gide. In the case of Valéry, you note his allegiance to Mallarmé's pure poetic principles, as well as to the Third Republic. In the case of Gide, you claim that, like Mallarmé, he posited "the void as the secret nothingness of prose" (MT 80). While Gide may well have written accounts of the Congo or the Soviet Union, he clearly stated that works like *Retour de l'URSS* "have almost no relation with literature"[4]. He thereby separated literature from worldly affairs. How do you see the specific relationship between Mallarmé and his disciples? Do Gide and Valéry bring the deleterious aspects of Mallarmé's doctrine into the twentieth century or do they inflect and displace it, whether in a positive or negative direction?

JCM: Whatever Mallarmé's final position on the Book, it seems evident to me that his two closest disciples saw it as an admirable venture, but one that was in vain. They drew the following conclusion from it: *one does not create institutions*. Valéry considered that it was necessary to stick to existing institutions, organized literature, journals, the Third Republic, the Collège de France, *l'Académie française*, etc. Not because he respected them, but because he despised them. Gide considered, on the contrary, that it was necessary to undermine institutions, to expose their lines of weakness. His homosexuality drove him to it—I note that it was once held to be a crime in most major democracies, except for France. Besides, he always preferred boys who were fifteen years old, which was then and still is a crime in France. But his gesture is of a greater scope and affects all institutional forms: the judicial system, French colonization, the Soviet system, etc. Literature is no exception: when Gide turns toward it, he ends up choosing prose because he discovered that prose *and not poetry* is the true writing of nothingness. I refer to *Voyage d'Urien* and to *Paludes*. If, moreover, he wrote texts that have almost no relation to literature; if he accorded such importance to his journal, which, in principle, is not an official literary form; if, in this journal—for a Mallarméan, the choice of this name is meaningful—he treats literary works as a personal pastime, then the result comes down to undermining the status of literature in society and the French state apparatus. *La Nouvelle Revue Française (NRF)* could pass as a counterexample, but precisely Gide distanced himself from it as it became an institution. Moreover, after the war, it is through the intermediary of Jacques Rivière that Proust will annex the *NRF* and rule over Gallimard. Only the premature death of Rivière and Proust will conceal this sort of coup d'état. Whatever the case may be, Valéry and Gide represent two opposite faces of the same renunciation of the Book.

But it will be said that Mallarmé also abandoned the Book, at least in my view. Certainly, but precisely, Valéry and Gide did not understand or know this. As all disciples do, it appealed to them to assume that their Master had gone astray, that he was as naive as a child, and that it was up to them to show that they were grown-ups. They thought that Mallarmé believed in the Book until the end. Their renunciation is therefore in no way comparable to Mallarmé's final gesture. Instead of concluding, as he did, in the nothingness of institutions, whether these exist or are to be created, they consent to the positivity of existing institutions, one in order to consolidate them, the other in order to undermine them.

RB & CG: In your work on French intellectual life and on the institutions that gave it a brief flickering of light during the Third Republic, you make some intriguing remarks about *NRF*. You say that the *NRF* was "a system of oasis in the French desert" (EVI 18) since it was an attempt—analogical to that of the creation of the University under the Third Republic—to create an autonomous sphere of intellectual production and a class of salaried professionals of knowledge. Given that some of the founding members of the *NRF* were young disciples of Mallarmé, do you see any relation between his originally utopian vision—namely, that of the institution of the Book—and the kind of institution that his disciples Gide, Valéry, and Claudel were involved in creating in the case of the *NRF*? Certainly, you would hold that the *NRF* was, like the very phenomenon of intellectual life in France, an exception and thus an oasis. But what lessons might we nevertheless draw from its existence today?

JCM: I believe to the contrary that the creation of the *NRF* was born from an admission of failure—not only of the Book but also of the *Mardis* of the rue de Rome. Today we have forgotten to what degree the republican form of government inspired rejection on the part of writers and artists. The *Journal des Goncourt* testifies to this. The triumph of the middle class was accompanied, it seemed to them, by a glorification of mediocrity in art. Realism, as a literary and artistic doctrine, appeared to them simply as a literary reprise of bourgeois utilitarianism. The requirement for success transformed the writer into a literary merchant. Descriptive realism defined a form of profitability: literature can yield a profit, on the condition that it faithfully describes reality. As both a journal and a collection, the *NRF* wanted to offer a space where writers (and not booksellers) judged other writers, where the reciprocal esteem of writers was worth more than sales, where style and analysis outweighed description. In fact, the project is overtly aristocratic and antidemocratic, all the while accepting that society, in its entirety, is petty bourgeois and democratic. The *NRF* thinks of itself as an exception, certainly, but this exception confirms that the rule is precisely *l'inférieur clapotis quelconque*. While utopians want to change the rule, the *NRF* maintains it. From this point of view, it takes its place in a movement that the historians of the Third Republic have sometimes neglected and that, once again, the Goncourt had noted: after the first generation of republicans, born of 1848 and Hugolian in temperament, a new generation came to power that had not known 1848 and had abandoned Hugo to the little people. It wanted to develop, while respecting the general democratic rule, zones of aristocratic operation, the *grandes écoles* and the University for example. In other words, it did not want to leave to the antirepublican strata the monopoly of aristocratic values. This political program lasted. De Gaulle and all of the Gaullists implemented it and, paradoxically, the communists recognized themselves in it. It was swept away by May '68 and nobody in France understands it today. This is why, for example, contemporary

French society literally does not know what to make of its writers. It does not have a model other than the *NRF* at its disposal, but this model has become opaque to it.

What lessons can be drawn from this today? Your question is of little interest if it only concerns France. I thus consider that it concerns a transnational space. Say, the space of the global market. The technique of the oasis is not bad, on the condition that the oases connect with each other in a network. They do not speak the same language; therefore, there immediately arises the problem of translation [*translation*]—I prefer the English word to the French *traduction*. These problems are not new in themselves. Cicero encountered them between Greece and Rome, but they are being posed under new conditions.

There certainly exists a global language, which is English, but insofar as it is global, it is not a language; it not only stands in the way of other languages, but above all it explodes the English language itself. To overcome the difficulty, we can transform the problem into a solution. What is said in French or Chinese or Swahili can allow English speaking subjects to hear once more the linguistic dimension [*dimension de langue*] of their own language. The French language is on the way to becoming a dead one, in the sense that nothing new can be said in it; more exactly, a new proposition in French is neither heard nor understood, neither by French subjects nor by the others. The various languages—English, German, African or Asian languages—can awaken what has become inert. The translators play an important role in this translation [*translation*], but they are not the only ones.

RB & CG: What may surprise your readers is that one of your most recent books was on the political significance of the Harry Potter films.[5] In contrast to *Mallarmé au tombeau*, which analyses the specifically French uptake of the poet's ideals and political program, you turn to Harry Potter in order to think through its uniquely British take on politics, intersubjective tolerance, and the post-Thatcherite political situation. For you, while contemporary thought should leave behind Mallarmé's political vision of the world, the Harry Potter films offer a series of progressive political lessons and directives for us today. In your analysis, what is the political kernel of the Harry Potter films, and do you see a productive relationship between the British "Potterian narrative" and contemporary France? In other words, do the Harry

Potter films speak to the political tradition dealt with in *Constats* and *Mallarmé au tombeau?*

JCM: As you point out, the Potterian narrative seems specifically British to me. But this characteristic depends on a very singular situation. Great Britain is confronted with a choice: it can become a kind of nth state of the USA—a kind of less sunny Hawaii—or it can continue to be an autonomous centre of English language culture, thanks to its institutions, its political thought, its artistic and literary creation. This choice seems to me much more dramatic than the question of membership in the Eurozone.[6] In the film *The Queen* (2006), I was struck by the nature of what was at stake. The cult of Princess Diana, Tony Blair's entourage, and the press push towards a complete integration of the British imaginary with the imaginary of the United States; Tony Blair himself and the Queen are opposed to this and will base their political alliance on this refusal. It is evident that the Potterian narrative shares the same refusal. It is not even evident that the American continent belongs to the wizards' geography.[7] The latter appears to be limited to the ensemble of the European continent (the Slavic world included) and to the Commonwealth, with Great Britain at the centre.

This highlighting of Great Britain has a political signification. According to J.K. Rowling, British culture is founded on tolerance; among the so-called democratic cultures, it is the only one to have given itself this foundation. While the American Revolution is, as is said, founded on freedom rather than equality and the French Revolution on equality rather than freedom, and while the societies born from these two revolutions do not succeed in resolving the difference between these two values, the British system would reconcile them in a third, which is tolerance.

This being admitted, for my part I hold that the debate is unwarranted. Freedom and equality are principles radically distinct from their empirical accomplishments; the major question concerns the junction between the idea and reality. You will recognize here a very Mallarméan style of questioning. Tolerance does not at all obey the same model: I would say that at bottom, tolerance does not exist, there are only gestures of tolerance. Moreover, I do not believe that the word is pronounced in the narrative—it is J.K. Rowling who employs it in a commentary on her own conception. She wants her narrative to carry its readers and spectators towards tolerance, not by speeches but by narrated events.

In terms of tolerance, the distinction between the idea and its realization does not apply. Tolerance has for its site *l'inférieur clapotis quelconque*; more exactly, the inferior/superior distinction is meaningless, the splashing/music distinction is meaningless, the anonymous/determined distinction is meaningless. We are far from Mallarmé.

Mallarmé does not hesitate to make allusions to magic, to the *grimoire*, to alchemy. He would perhaps have read J.K. Rowling with as much pleasure as he read Jules Verne, but I do not think that he would have been interested in her politics. There remains the relation to language. The author of *Les mots anglais* would, I believe, have been interested by the formation of a common noun such as *quidditch* and its possible relation to the *quidditas* of the scholastics; likewise, he would have been interested in the formation of proper names such as *Slytherin* or *Hufflepuff*. The relation between the Germanic, Latin, and French roots of modern English would equally have awakened his curiosity. Finally, he would perhaps have noted that, once again, Great Britain resisted what he called the "hyperscientific"[8] movement; but he would also have noted that in this case, it was not the belief in God that played the determining role but another, fundamentally Pagan belief at once anterior and indifferent to Christ.

ENGAGEMENTS, DISAGREEMENTS, AND METHODS OF READING

RB & CG: In *Mallarmé au tombeau*, you argue that the poet believed the world to be nothing more than the space and time of mere fashion, of the production of ephemeral commodities, and therefore of "material splendor and spiritual sterility" (MT 42). For him, poetry was eternally above and beyond this realm and thus radically distinct from prose. By contrast in *The Politics of the Siren*, Jacques Rancière argues that this prosaic world was the very matter of poetry for Mallarmé. Rancière claims that Mallarmé consequently could not draw a strict line of distinction between poetry and prose. His expansive definition of poetry is captured in the famous phrase: "the form we call verse is simply itself literature; that there is verse as soon as diction calls attention to itself, rhythm as soon as there is style" (D 202—*modified trans.*). How do you understand those readings of Mallarmé that insist upon the indistinction he seems to establish between the high and the low, the spiritual and the mundane, poetry and prose? How can we sustain the idea that Mallarmé placed his poetry at the height of "the Idea, eternally distinct and distant from any matter" (MT 63) when much of his corpus is made up of circumstantial pieces, journalistic sketches and critical poems that reflect on the current affairs of his time?

JCM: Rancière's book rests on a double confusion. For Mallarmé, anything can be the occasion for poetry—anything, that is to say, any circumstance, whether social or intimate or even, as some have suggested, a physiological episode. But if so, it is precisely because there is no relation between worldly reality and Literature. Literature or Letters make no distinction between what is or is not important in the *clapotis quelconque*. They are in exception to their occasion. The erection of a monument to Poe is the occasion for a sonnet, but it is not the subject of the sonnet. Yes, the everyday world offers an infinity of occasions, but this is because Literature judges them all to be of equal value since they are all null. Literature is committed to not confusing its occasion with its subject. Rancière has confused them. We cannot imagine a more complete misinterpretation.

As for the quote you reprise, it must be read in its context in "Crisis of Verse": "A monument in the desert, surrounded by silence; in a crypt, the divinity of a majestic unconscious idea—that is, that the form we call verse is simply itself literature; that there is verse as soon as diction calls attention to itself, rhythm as soon as there is style" (D 202—*modified trans.*). This is Victor Hugo. Mallarmé is paying tribute to him, but by making a statue of him that is as abandoned as the divinity of an ancient cult. We can think of the gods of Carthage such as Flaubert described them. Nobody believes in these gods anymore.

The majestic idea is the idea that the Hugolian project implies and of which Hugo was unaware. Mallarmé abandoned precisely this. "There is verse as soon as diction calls attention to itself"; there is "rhythm as soon as there is style," the final indistinction of verse and prose, all of this develops Hugo's implicit program. For his part, Mallarmé takes the exact opposite view. By inversion, each sentence should thus allow us to restore the Mallarméan proposition:

(a) Verse is not equivalent to Literature; it adds something specific to Literature
(b) There is no Verse as soon as diction is accentuated.

(c) Yes, verse outlines a rhythm, but this rhythm has nothing to do with style.
(d) Style is not enough. In fact, style is proper to prose and there is no style in poetry.
(e) Prose and poetry are radically different.

Rancière has taken for an identification the proclamation of an irreducible difference. He attributes to Mallarmé a position that Mallarmé himself is only summarizing and that he rejects. Once again, we cannot imagine a more complete misinterpretation.

RB & CG: In your 1992 book *Constat*, you analyze the discursive space of the political vision of the world and affirm its undoing at the moment of the downfall of the USSR. Consequently, you argue against those who refuse to "pose the questions of the dénounement" and who therefore think "nothing has taken place" (CO 61). Among those who are convinced that "nothing has taken place," you seem to count Alain Badiou. In his 1991 essay *Of an Obscure Disaster*, for example, Badiou holds that the swift and spectacular crumbling of the Soviet bloc revealed no profound novelty, but was merely the miserable coda to political transformations that had long since taken place. Furthermore, Badiou argues that "the USSR, gray despotic totality, a reversal of October into its opposite"[9] had never even been a proper instance of Communist politics. Despite implying that he "counted among the major spirits of that time" (CO 59), *Constat* is directed against Badiou's assessment. Given that *Mallarmé au tombeau* also seems to be implicated in this assessment of two centuries of revolutionary politics, could you explain the context in which your work *Constat* was written, specifically as it bears upon your discord with Badiou?

JCM: I will limit myself to *Constat*.[10] At that time, between Badiou and I there was not really a disagreement about the facts, but an opposition as to their interpretation. For my part, I questioned the idea of revolution itself; as this idea had governed thinking, notably in France, it presented a certain number of distinctive traits. I tried to summarize them in *Constat*, making use of the notions of infinity and the maximum: since the French Revolution, revolution promised the intersection, at an infinite point, of the will and thought. This intersection was to be obtained by the intensification, to their maximal degree, of the will and thought.

Regarding the facts, I granted entirely to Badiou that this idea had for a long time been refuted by what was happening in the USSR. But, in its representations, it remained entirely active and notably so when the name of Lenin was pronounced. After all, the leftism of the 70s could vary on many points, but not on the definition of Lenin as a major revolutionary. If I remember correctly, even in 1989 Badiou did not say that Lenin embodied the reversal of October into its opposite. With the fall of the statues of Lenin I perceived that in an instant October 17 itself was undermined: since October was Lenin—and since Lenin had been laid low—either October had never been a revolution (but then the twentieth century would rest on an error) or October had been an authentic revolution (but then the notion of revolution itself was void). In both cases, I considered that something significant had taken place in the form of a disappearance: henceforth politics would no longer be determined by the maximality of thought or will, nor by the coincidence between will and thought, nor by the interpretation of maximality in terms of infinity. There was a movement towards definitions of politics in terms of minimality, of finitude, and of the noncoincidence between thought and will.

In "Logical Time," Lacan stages three prisoners: based on what he sees in the other two, each must determine the colour of the sign he carries on his back, which he does not see. Lacan separates the moment of the gaze, where the subject considers the colours he has before his eyes, and the moment of conclusion, where the subject defines his own colour. It seems to me that the disagreement between Badiou and myself plays this out. The fall of the statues and the end of the USSR taught us nothing, neither him nor me, because we had long since concluded; what he and I had in common was that we had seen what the Chinese had been pointing to. He deduced from this that the end of the Soviet bloc objectively revealed nothing new. To this I opposed and still oppose today the idea that this does not hold for the other prisoners. They looked, but they did not conclude. The fall of the statues forced them to conclude. This moment of conclusion for all was what was new.

You will notice that this disagreement is reminiscent of our disagreement about Plato's Cave: Badiou holds that the prisoners should and must exit the cave—this would suffice to solve Lacan's fable, if we imagined that it takes place in Plato's cave. In the sun of the Good, the time of conclusion is immediately contemporary with each instant of the gaze. For my part, nobody can or should exit the Cave, simply because there is no exterior to it; the moment of conclusion is disjoined from the instance of the gaze until a final visible event forces the conclusion.

RB & CG: In *Constats*, the phrase "nothing has taken place" clearly applies to those who, like Badiou, held that nothing that took place during the downfall of the Soviet bloc could force thought to reconsider the revolutionary history played out between 1789 and 1989. The phrase is a marker of what you call "the highest fidelity" (CO 61) that Badiou has to this revolutionary tradition. In *Mallarmé au tombeau*, however, the phrase reflects what Mallarmé himself thought of this tradition. As you put it more recently in *L'Universel en éclats* (2013), the poet held that "nothing of the 19th century had taken place: not 1815, not 1830, not June 1848, not Napoleon III, nor the Commune" (UE 31). In other words, Mallarmé stands for an extreme nihilist denial of any and all revolutionary events. How do you understand the relation between the poet's nihilism and Badiou's revolutionary fidelity?

JCM: "Nothing has taken place but the place" is equivocal. I confess that I enjoyed playing on it. In *Constat* and *Mallarmé au tombeau*, the phrase "nothing has taken place" refers to two precisely opposed choices. But their foundation is the same: the decision of indifference with respect to what happens in the *l'inférieur clapotis*. My position is the opposite: nothing that takes place merits indifference, whether in the inferior splashing or in the superior music; everything makes a difference, everything is an event. You oppose the nihilism I ascribe to Mallarmé with Badiou's revolutionary fidelity. I could note that in both cases, it is a question of fidelity: fidelity to the nothing, on the one hand, and fidelity to such and such an event, on the other. It would not be very difficult for me to construct a discourse where these two fidelities would appear equivalent. On this point also, I distinguish myself. Fidelity, for me, is not a virtue. To refute oneself is a symptom of the truth.

RB & CG: Following Bertrand Marchal and Jacques Rancière, Quentin Meillassoux's recent interpretation of Mallarmé's *Un coup de dés* argues that the purpose of the poem was to found a civic religion without God. Unlike Marchal and Rancière, however, Meillassoux's analysis pushes Mallarmé's project one step further, positing the poem as the single exception to the failed projects of nineteenth century modernity. Having retrospectively discovered a secular Eucharist in the poem that sublated, in a rigorously atheist fashion, the Christian religion of the past, Meillassoux frames his reading of the *Coup de dés* as an unapologetic defence of the utopian and revolutionary project of modernity. If, as you claim, after 1991 we have entered into a new political era that moves us away from past revolutionary projects and practices, how would you understand a contemporary reading of *Un coup de dés* that draws its force from the discursive parameters of the political vision of the world?

JCM: These interpretations seem to me to neglect explicit remarks by Mallarmé, which, moreover, I cited in *Mallarmé au tombeau*. To this, I have since added other reasons for rejecting them. In particular, I believe that the death of Anatole, the lost son, plays an infinitely more important role than has been supposed and still traverses the *Coup de dés*. In fact, I believe that the *Coup de dés* is not a fulfilment of the Book, but a fulfilment of *Tombeau d'Anatole*. In my view, Mallarmé was confronted with a dilemma: either the Book or the *Tombeau d'Anatole*. He ended by choosing the second. But deep down this is of no importance: I could accept Meillassoux's interpretation and not accept, however, the lessons he draws for the present. Even if Mallarmé thought that with the *Coup de dés* he had given new arms to politics, I think we cannot go against the following fact: nobody, not even him, neither by the imagination nor by thought, could have foreseen what the twentieth century would bring. Before the experience of it had taken place, none of the greatest minds of the past could have known what we know man and technology are capable of today. If you have read *Les penchants criminels de l'Europe démocratique* (2003) you know what I am thinking about.[11] If the *Coup de dés* thus involves a utopia (something I do not believe), this utopia signifies nothing for the present or for the future.

RB & CG: At the end of *Mallarmé au tombeau*, you frame our contemporary predicament as that of finding a way between, on the one hand, the extreme nihilism of a poetry like Mallarmé's and, on the other hand, the mediocrity of journalism. Just like Mallarmé you also decry "the newspaper in its most impoverished form: the language of numbers and names" (MT 85). What is required, you argue, is a form of prose that navigates between these two equally inadequate modes of writing. In the almost twenty years since the publication of *Mallarmé au tombeau*, what prose works have taken up the challenge of finding a third way between poetry and journalism? Does Chalamov, for instance, still remain a model to emulate? Would you articulate our contemporary predicament in terms of the poetry/prose distinction today?

JCM: Basically, you are asking me for the names of authors. I am not here to distribute prizes. Why does Chalamov count for me? For one reason: he treated the Kolyma, of which he had the most direct experience, like Flaubert treated Carthage. The Kolyma narratives are a modern *Salammbô*. But you measure the unprecedented nature of the effort, since it must speak of what takes place for oneself, as if one had not been there—thus, journalism is avoided; but this annihilation of presence must also create a truth-effect: *nothing has taken place but the place, but the place has taken place, I am its effect*. Regarding analogous efforts, I know of some in French language prose today. I know of some in other languages too. If you would like the names I can give them, but should we ever give names?

RB & CG: Over the course of your prolific career, Mallarmé has appeared in a number of seminal moments, taking the role of both enemy and friend, deplorable nihilist or exemplar of certain linguistic theses. In your work, his poetry has been in a dialogue with Lacan, with modern science, and with politics—but, above all, your work has put the poet into a unique conversation with language itself. How would you summarize your relationship with the poet? How have Mallarmé's constellations guided your thought? And lastly, what role, if any, will the poet play in your current or future work?

JCM: After *Mallarmé au tombeau*, I kept myself at a distance. I noticed the works that were being undertaken carefully ignored my own. The only thing to do in a desert is to change places. Thus, I went elsewhere, no doubt to find other deserts. Recently, I have returned to Mallarmé. I discovered other dice games and new connections with language. I think notably of the terrible game he played with the death of his son and of anagrams, in the lineage of Saussure and Jakobson. More generally, his *œuvre*—poetry and prose—again forms the heart of my work. To take just one example, recent events have led me to reflect on the crowd; in what sense did the attacks of January 2015 in Paris enter into a relation with the phenomenon of the crowd? Did those who march against these attacks form a crowd? And those who killed? And those who were killed? If yes, is this a crowd that declares itself, as per Mallarmé's expression? If not, what is it? Analogous questions occupied Mallarmé. The fragments he left behind on this subject are of the greatest importance for me. This does not mean that I adhere to them. Basically, I would willingly take up for my own purposes Paul Claudel's expression: Mallarmé, *professeur d'attention*.

NOTES

1. Jean-Claude Milner, "Prose Redeemed," trans. John Cleary, *S: Journal for the Circle of Lacanian Ideology Critique*, Vol 3 (2010): 106–113.

2. We have decided to retain Mallarmé's original French, as opposed to a standard translation, which would be 'some splashing below'. The reason for this is that the English does not capture the two adjectival meanings of 'inférieur', as both a topological descriptor and a value laden term, nor does it deliver the sense of mediocrity or anonymity implied by 'quelconque'. [*TN.*]

3. "Tout pour moi devient allégorie"

4. André Gide, *Journal 1939–1949* (Paris: Gallimard, 1955), 322. Cited in *Camarade Mallarmé*, 39.

5. Jean-Claude Milner, *Harry Potter : A l'école des sciences morales et politiques* (Paris: PUF, 2014).

6. This interview took place in June, 2015—a year before the Brexit referendum.

7. This interview took place in June, 2015—a year and a half before *Fantastic Beasts and Where to Find Them* (2016) was released.

8. Stéphane Mallarmé, *Œuvre Complètes I*, 872–873.

9. Alain Badiou, *D'un dèsastre obscur. Droit, Etat, Politique* (Paris: L'Aube, 1992) 14.

10. For a partial translation of this work, see Jean-Claude Milner, "The Revolution, Infinite Conjunction," trans. Tzuchien Tho, *S: Journal for the Circle of Lacanian Ideology Critique*, Vol 3 (2010): 64–69.

11. For a partial translation of this work, see Jean-Claude Milner, "The Traps of the All," trans. Ed Pluth, *S: Journal for the Circle of Lacanian Ideology Critique*, Vol 3 (2010): 22–39.

Chapter Three

"Mallarmé Said It All"

Alain Badiou

MALLARMÉ, MATHEMATICS, AND THE RED YEARS

Robert Boncardo & Christian R. Gelder: During the 1960s—roughly the same time that you yourself starting contributing to public discussion—there was an increased interest in Mallarmé, particularly within literary theoretical circles around avant-garde journals such as *Change* and *Tel Quel*. In these circles, Mallarmé's poetry and prose was seen to resonate with key structuralist concerns, including the impersonality of language, its resistance to reference, and the search for a scientific definition of literariness or poetic language. There was also an attempt to link these concerns with an avant-gardist or revolutionary politics, such as the debate that occurred between Jean-Pierre Faye and Philippe Sollers in 1969 over *le camarade Mallarmé*. From your perspective, what was the significance of Mallarmé in French intellectual circles during the late 1960s and early 1970s? In terms of your own trajectory, what were your first encounters with the poet?

Alain Badiou: It would be more appropriate to speak of there being a new content to the interest in Mallarmé, rather than a new interest in him *per se*. Don't forget that a typical representative of the previous generation, namely Sartre, was fascinated by Mallarmé, and spent his whole life working on a book devoted to him. Mallarmé was fundamental for Blanchot or, in another domain, for Boulez, even before the period 1965–1975, a period defined by the domination of structuralism, and then by a desire for revolution—a period that I have called "the Red Years." What happens in this period, which is the one you are referring to, is that Mallarmé is included in the genealogy of structuralism, in something of a transcendental conception of language, linguistics, semiotics, and also in the eradication of the notion of the Subject (the poem "takes place all by itself" (D 219)). For my part, as I came out of Sartre, I was in some sense able to traverse the two Mallarmés: the Mallarmé who fascinates Sartre and Blanchot through the motifs of Nothingness, Silence, and Anxiety, and the Mallarmé who fascinates *Tel Quel* or the *Cahiers pour l'analyse* through the joint motifs of the powerful neutrality of language and the operational void that is the Subject. This possible traversal of the two different Mallarmés was facilitated—in fact more than facilitated—by the work of Gardner Davies. In truth, I owe him for having been the first to approach Mallarmé outside of any mystery with a conviction in his profound rationality—a rationality that could just as well have originated in Sartre (there is a "vanishing subject" in Mallarmé, whose entire being lies in Nothingness), as in structuralism (this subject is the active void of a linguistic order). I synthesized my own reading of Mallarmé in a course given at the Collège Universitaire de Reims during the academic year of 1967–68. This course focused on Mallarmé, Rimbaud, and Lautréamont. The brutal beginning of the May '68 movement made Lautréamont disappear and catapulted me into Maoist action. However, at the end of the 1970s, when I again took up the thread that I had drawn from the *Coup de dés*, I found it intact. It is this thread that directs the reading of Mallarmé proposed in my *Theory of the Subject* (1982).

RB & CG: In "Mark and Lack," your seminal contribution to the final edition of the *Cahiers pour l'analyse*, you argue that mathematical science does not follow the logic of the signifier and its articulated concepts of lack, foreclosure, suture, and so on—*pace* what Jacques-Alain Miller had attempted to demonstrate in his equally seminal "Suture." At a crucial moment in your argument, you affirm the integrally rule-governed nature of mathematical science, its strict universality, and consequently its absolute foreclosure of the particularities of the individual subject who might deploy it. You then argue that it is therefore only mathematics that can effectively obey the Mallarméan injunction to impersonality: "If one wants to exhibit writing as such, and to excise its author; if one wants to follow Mallarmé in enjoining the written work to occur with neither subject nor Subject, there is a way of doing this that is radical, secular, and exclusive of every other: by entering into the writings of science, whose law consists precisely in this" (ML 172 n. 24). Paradoxically, then, it seems that it is only by stepping *outside* of poetry and *into* mathematics that one can effect "the disappearance of the poet speaking" (D 208). Can you elaborate on how, at the time of the *Cahiers*, you understood the intersections and disjunctions between Mallarmé and mathematics?

AB: For me, Mallarmé represents the person who launched a poetic challenge to mathematics by assuming that the rigour of poetic language could equal the rigour of mathematics, but moreover also assumed the power of Chance, something mathematics cannot do. It is for this reason that the possibility of Igitur's act brings forth the victorious cry, "You mathematicians, expired." When, later on, I made the event the key to the upsurge of truths, I in fact integrated this Mallarméan doctrine in the following form: mathematics thinks being as such, being *qua* being, but cannot integrate the aleatory notion of the possible that is conveyed by the event. The effective sign of this point is that the event suspends a fundamental axiom of the mathematical theory: the axiom of foundation. This upsurge of the unfounded obviously finds its poetic symbol in Mallarmé's *Coup de dés*. It is thus here that, as the agent of the consequences of the event, the individual can become a subject. However, in the 1960s, I was fundamentally concerned with the significance of mathematics, and therefore with the asubjective force of its process, without yet opening up the theory of the possibility of an event and its generic consequences, namely truths. Fundamentally, at this time, I was already struggling against a purely structural theory of the subject, which made the subject the empty or void point of the structure, and which was largely that of Lacan and, in the *Cahiers pour l'analyse*, of Jacques-Alain Miller. When I say that mathematics forecloses the subject, I am preparing without knowing it the idea that for the subject to be, the structure must at one of its points be broken by an event. The formidable political shock of the Red Years will be necessary for me to see clearly on this point.

RB & CG: From the circumstantial, militant writings produced under the auspices of the UCFML, to the seminar you held at Vincennes University and which would go on to constitute *Theory of the Subject*, throughout the 1970s you consistently refer to Mallarmé as a great dialectician. In "The Current Situation on the Philosophical Front," for instance, you claim that Mallarmé is "the only productive Hegelian of our dominant national tradition of thought" (AFP 12). Such a surprising denomination forms part of the broader philosophical project you were pursuing at the time, namely, to renew dialectical thinking and thereby reinvigorate Marxism. What did it mean for you to draw on Mallarmé as a resource for a specifically political thinking during this time? How did you understand your appropriation of Mallarmé with respect to other readings produced within a Maoist orientation, such as those of *Tel Quel?*

AB: The central philosophical question for the Maoism of this time was the question of the dialectic. During the 1960s, this question had already pitted the Chinese communists, who argued that the active heart of dialectical thought was that "One divides into two," against the Soviet communists who, in order to justify their politics of "peaceful coexistence" with American imperialism, supported the formula "Two fuse into One." Now, it is clear that Mallarmé supports division against fusion: at the end of the *Coup de dés*, there is clearly, on the one hand, "these latitudes of indeterminate waves in which all reality dissolves [*les parages du vague où toute réalité se dissout*]," and on the other hand, if the poem is victorious (and it can only "perhaps" be victorious), there is a Constellation, which means an Idea. I therefore simply thought that, in the register of the poem, Mallarmé was on the side of Mao. But I have never fused poetry and politics: for me, they are distinct truth procedures. The positions of *Tel Quel* always seemed confused to me, and above all fragile. We can see this fragility clearly now that all of the leaders of the time who have reneged on their political engagements from the 1970s, now participate in the anticommunist consensus, and have become vulgar "democrats."

RB & CG: Turning to your engagement with Mallarmé in *Theory of the Subject*, the poet seems to occupy an ambivalent position in the book. On the one hand, his patience and intransigence encapsulate the political endurance required by the Maoist militants during what you name, evoking "Sonnet en -yx," "the anxiety of the night of imperialist societies" (TS 108). On the other hand, you read him as an exemplary thinker of the structural dialectic, which you purport to circumscribe and transcend in the direction of an historical dialectic. Mallarmé inscribes a series of operations that the Maoist militants must pass beyond if they are to think political change in the direction of communism. You even go so far as to suggest that, despite the radicality of his poetic operations and his recognition of the primacy of strong difference, Mallarmé was actually an incurable conservative for whom "there is no temporal advent of the new" (TS 108). How did your reading of Mallarmé in *Theory of the Subject* develop? Would you agree that Mallarmé is treated somewhat ambivalently in this book, as opposed to the unequivocally positive treatment he receives in *Being and Event?*

AB: An entire section of *Theory of the Subject* does indeed aim to distinguish clearly between the structural dialectic (which is centred on what I call the Splace) and the historical dialectic (which is centred on what I call the Outplace). Mathematically, this opposes algebra to topology. Subjectively, this opposes the couple Anxiety/Superego to the couple Courage/Justice. I present Mallarmé as a great master of the structural dialectic, which without any doubt he is: a poem by Mallarmé always deals with what is lacking-in-its-place in a structured place. And he describes the conditions of anxiety, in the night of the disappearance of the sun. At the time, however, I had not yet established the category of the event. My reading of Mallarmé was therefore unilateral. I did not see that beyond structure and lack (which are Lacanian categories) there is, in a number of his poems, the possibility given by Chance, and that there is therefore an opening in the dialectical division of the place on the basis of a radical event. This is what I later brought to light in *Being and Event.*

BEING AND EVENT AND THE DOCTRINE OF CONDITIONS

RB & CG: While in *Theory of the Subject* you move between Mallarmé, mathematics, Maoism, Ancient Greek theatre, and the French political scene without distinguishing these discourses in terms of their singularity, in *Being and Event* and *Manifesto for Philosophy* you propose a strict separation between philosophy and its four conditions: art, science, politics, and love. In this new doctrine, philosophy has the exclusive task of constructing a contemporary thinking of truth, being, and the subject that can *compossibilize* the truths effectively produced in these four absolutely autonomous domains. In terms of the intraphilosophical inscription of these conditions, mathematics thinks being, while poetry, specifically Mallarmé, thinks the event, without there being any transitivity between the two. The doctrine of conditions involves, then, the philosopher having to rework their own operations under the pressure of novel productions in these domains: for instance, Mallarmé's *Un coup de dés* constitutes "the greatest theoretical text that exists on the conditions for thinking the event" (IE 74). Can you elaborate on what it is about poetry, and the poetry of Mallarmé in particular, that makes it singularly capable of thinking the event?

AB: It is necessary to understand that poetry and mathematics—poem and matheme—constitute the two extremes of language. To the greatest degree possible, mathematics constitutes an exception to the particularity of national (or maternal) languages. It is therefore appropriate for directly grasping the general laws of being, for symbolically coding a complete theory of any multiplicity whatsoever. On the contrary, poetry enters deeply into the singularity of languages and seeks a hidden kernel of universality *in this singularity*. As such, poetry is more appropriate to the event—to the nomination of the event—since the event is always localized in a determinate situation or world. Poetry can accompany the movement of the event towards its universal consequences, which strike a particular situation, while mathematics can better grasp the immutability of ontology's laws.

RB & CG: In the essay "Mallarmé's Method," you write that the poet offers us a "thought-poem of the event in its undecidability" (C 298). Throughout the reception of his work, and in particular of *Un coup de dés*, numerous interpretations of undecidability have been proposed, from Derrida to Meillassoux. For you, this concept is linked to the relation of belonging between the event and the situation of its upsurge. In *Un coup de dés*, you discern a metaphorical evocation of this precarious, undecidable status of the event. In our view, this reading of undecidability also appears to be linked to the mathematical procedure of forcing, where an undecidable statement in an initial situation *will have been decided* in the generic extension. Given, then, that there appears to be a close, consistent relation between the procedure of forcing and the category of undecidability in *Un coup de dés*, is it plausible to say that the philosopher must make the intraphilosophical contributions of mathematics and poetry interlock? Is the intraphilosophical inscription of Mallarmé's poetry irreducibly mediated by the mathematics, specifically by the procedure of forcing?

AB: Yes, the concept of the generic, insofar as it characterizes the being of a truth, is in a sense poetico-mathematical. It is "poetic" insofar as it is that which is added to a singular situation on the basis of the spark of the event; it is mathematical insofar as it can be captured in its universality as a particular type of multiplicity. We can say the following: the generic subset of a particular multiplicity is poetic insofar as it goes from the particularity to the universal that this particularity contains. It is mathematical insofar as the law of its construction can be formalized in a directly universal way, such that we can also go from the universal to the particular, from the general definition of forcing to the determination of a generic extension that has such and such a particular property.

RB & CG: In an occasional essay published in *Handbook of Inaesthetics* entitled "A French Philosopher responds to a Polish Poet," you defend Mallarmé and modern French poetry from a series of critiques leveled against them by the Polish Nobel Laureate, Czeslaw Milosz. In his book *The Witness of Poetry* (1983), Milosz argued that ever since the Symbolists, French poetry has retreated into a restricted, aristocratic, or even individualistic sphere cut off from the large mass of people, thereby renouncing its proper post-Romantic duty: to speak to the "Human Family."[1] Against Milosz, you argue that Mallarmé not only recuses individualism via his doctrine of impersonality, but also that he addresses his poetry to a figure of generic humanity, which he calls the Crowd. Furthermore, you make the broader claim that "[t]he poem is, in an exemplary way, destined to all" (HI 41). How do you understand the relation between Mallarmé's poetry and universality? What does the figure of the Crowd name, as you understand it?

AB: Romantic poetry subordinated universality to sentimental personal experience. As Hugo would have said: "Foolish are you who think that I am not you! [*Insensé, qui crois que je ne suis pas toi!*]." By contrast, Mallarmé grounds universality in the transcendence of identities and not in their supposed fusion. His goal is in some sense to establish the rules for a universal communication, which would bear upon an ideal object and to which an impersonal subject would be linked via operations of subtraction. This process is aristocratic, if you wish, but in the sense that by refusing all identitarian psychology and all socially established positions it participates in what I have called a proletarian aristocratism. Or what the great artist of the theatre Antoine Vitez called an "elitism for all."

INFLUENCES AND INTERLOCUTORS

RB & CG: You have frequently expressed your debt to Gardner Davies, who in *Theory of the Subject* you call a "luminous analyst of Mallarmé" (TS 367). We can see the mark of Davies' reading in your understanding of *Un coup de dés* as a conceptual drama, which reaches a victorious conclusion at the moment the constellation appears, perhaps, on the final page of the poem. We might also suggest that the singularity of your reading, particularly with respect to other French readers from Valéry to Jean-Pierre Richard, owes much to the influence of Davies. How would you describe your philosophical, as well as personal, relations with Gardner Davies? More critically, while he presents Mallarmé as a systematic thinker whose basic operations correspond to a kind of Hegelianism, you explicitly reject the identification of his poetic operations with negation, writing in *Theory of the Subject* that "[t]he causality of lack," as we find it in Mallarmé, "has nothing to do with the labour of the negative" (TS 93). Is there an irreducible point of disagreement between yourself and Davies over Mallarmé's Hegelianism? Is there a point at which you pass beyond the "greatest interpreter of Mallarmé, the Australian Gardner Davies" (IE 69)?

AB: What I have retained from Gardner Davies is that the processes of the Mallarméan poem are not hermetic, but dialectical. In this respect, they are integrally rational. Beyond this, I differ from this great interpreter with respect to the dialectic itself. I believe that Gardner Davies remains largely on the side, not so much of Hegel, but of a structural dialectic, which does not give its proper place to the thought of the event as the originary point of a possible truth procedure. This dialectic seeks to "draw," in a unilateral manner, the poetic operations towards the side of the artifices of the negative.

RB & CG: In 1988, two pathbreaking, alternative readings of Mallarmé were proposed: your own reading of *Un coup de dés* in *Being and Event* and Bertrand Marchal's *La Religion de Mallarmé*. Since this date, Marchal's work has exerted an unprecedented level of influence in Mallarmé studies, reorienting our understanding of Mallarmé towards a vision of him as the creator of a civic religion in the lineage of other nineteenth-century utopians. Other philosophical readings of the poet, such as Rancière's, Lacoue-Labarthe's and Meillassoux's all appear to integrate something of Marchal's work into their own. However, in contrast to Marchal, your reading is extremely attentive to the minute operations of vanishing, annulment and foreclosure in *Un coup de dés*, "À la nue accablante tu" and "Sonnet en -yx", among other poems. How would you compare your reading of Mallarmé to Marchal's? Given your attentiveness to the Mallarméan problematic of the ceremony in *Five Lessons on Wagner* (2010), how do you conceive of the status of religion in the poet's work? Is there a relation between the centrality of the event and other Mallarméan themes such as religion, the ceremony, and the common?

AB: It is incontestable that Mallarmé wanted to compete with religion, notably Catholicism, at the level of what could be called a ceremony of the Absolute. But in itself this is not very interesting; it is a point of history, shared in fact by many nineteenth-century creators. All of this refers to the death of God. It should also be noted that this effort in the direction of a mimetic religion was a total failure. The Mallarméan ceremony does not exist. Moreover, the effort to create it does not form part of what is most active and alive in Mallarmé's legacy. Mallarmé subsists as a poet-thinker in the effective operations of his work—in other words, in his contribution to dialectical thought. I think that the passage from Gardner Davies to Marchal is a veritable historicist and academic regression.

RB & CG: Jacques Rancière's reading of Mallarmé closely engages with your own interpretation, while also developing themes found in Marchal's work. In the "Notes, Commentaries and Digressions" to *Logics of Worlds*, you praise his book *The Politics of the Siren*, yet note that you see nothing specifically political in the figure of the vanishing siren, which Rancière reads as a metonymy for Mallarmé's vision of poetry and its political vocation. Rather than writing a book entitled *The Politics of the Siren*, you remark that you would have written *The Ontology of the Siren*. What is the significance and force of Rancière's reading of Mallarmé for you? How do you understand the distinction between a politics, as opposed to an ontology, of the siren?

AB: Rancière shares with Marchal (and also with Milner, and even Sartre) the conviction that in order to understand Mallarmé we must refer to the political problems of his time, notably the failure of revolutions, and singularly those of June 1848 and the Paris Commune in 1871. A number of artists from this time were indeed dedicated to the possible transfiguration of these political failures into the form of a metaphorical "religion." In passing, I salute the effort that consists in deciphering their work in this light. It is a beautiful effort, but one I believe has been made in vain. Once again, Mallarmé's singularity lies entirely in what novelty the operations of thought-in-language that are his bring to dialectical thought in its complex relation between the poem and the matheme. The crucial image of the Siren certainly covers the subtle link between multiplicity, event, negation, and genericity. But what can we do and think with this material that would be directly "political"?

RB & CG: In what you call his "peculiar postlinguistic trajectory" (LW 522), Jean-Claude Milner crosses paths with Mallarmé in both 1992's *Constat* and 1999's *Mallarmé au tombeau*. Each book centres on an adaptation of a famous phrase from *Un coup de dés*: "Nothing has taken place but the place." In *Constat*, this refers to the conviction of those who, holding fast to the integrity of the Communist Idea, affirmed that "nothing took place in Moscow in 1991" (CO 11). In *Mallarmé au tombeau*, it encapsulates Milner's radical reinterpretation of Mallarmé as a counterrevolutionary who thought that 1830, 1848, and 1871 did not take place. Both books explicitly engage with you as a key interlocutor. Generally speaking, how do you understand Milner's postlinguistic work, particularly insofar as he treats the poet with a remarkable amount of detail? How would you respond to Milner's nihilist Mallarmé—a Mallarmé who is irreconcilable with your own?

AB: I do not think that Mallarmé was ever a nihilist. This interpretation is Milner's fable. I will take a sole example: a good part of his analysis bears upon the sonnet "Le vierge, le vivace et le bel aujourd'hui." But it just so happens that he does not even remark upon what is no doubt the most important point in it: in the first appearance of the swan—which is the central symbol of the whole poem, "A swan of former times remembers it is he" (PV 164)—we are indeed dealing with the bird, the swan, with a lowercase "s". But in its final appearance, as the last word of the sonnet and now with a capital letter—"the useless exile of the Swan" (PV 164)—it is the constellation of the Swan, with a capital

"S". Just as in the *Coup de dés*, when the disaster of the sunken ship is sublimated into a Constellation, the swan—and strictly speaking I am all for the idea that it is a question here of the poetico-revolutionary history of the Romantics, although I am not entirely sure of it—is only paralysed to the degree that it also transforms itself into a constellation, whose exile and uselessness cannot mask its eternity and glory. Milner's interpretation—because it is adialectical and in reality seeks to cover over and legitimize his own abandonment, from the middle of the 1970s onwards, of all of his post-May '68 Maoist fervour—completely misses the creative meaning of the Mallarméan poem, which exposes itself to the peril of nihilism only to dismiss it. RB & CG: In *A Short Treatise on Transitory Ontology*, you write that Mallarmé is "Cantor's unconscious contemporary" (TO 124) as both thinkers made the infinite a number. Moreover, since for you "modernity is defined by the fact that the One is not" (NN 65), Mallarmé and Cantor appear to be absolutely modern insofar as they place the infinite and the nothing at the heart of their discourses. In "The Tell-Tale Constellations," Milner draws on his understanding of post-Galilean mathematized science to suggest that the various images Mallarmé deploys—in particular, constellations—encapsulate a poetic exception to the Galilean universe, an exception that refers us to an older understanding of science, mathematics, and the cosmos, such as the Renaissance *liber mundi*. What implications, if any, does Milner's conception of post-Galilean science have for your understanding of both Mallarmé and mathematics?

AB: Again, I think that this is a very interesting, but unfounded, fable. On the contrary: what characterizes the Galilean-Newtonian universe is the fact that it introduced the infinite into the intelligibility of the world. Mallarmé absolutely integrates this modern dimension. The Constellation of the Swan is exiled and useless with respect to the finitude of our experience because, like the Great Bear from the *Coup de dés*, it is situated at the point where a "place" fuses with a "beyond" (CP 144), which is a good poetic definition of the infinite: we believe we can locate something in a fixed place, in the assured finitude of a position, but it is already beyond this stability. Just like Cantor, Mallarmé opens thought to an affirmative infinite. We see this quite explicitly in the text of *Igitur:* the act of throwing the dice, which brings chance into play, certainly implies the absurd, but prevents it from existing. Mallarmé concludes that this "permits the infinite to be." There is no better way of saying that the existence of the infinite is thought as the negation of nihilist absurdity. Galileo, Newton, Cantor, Mallarmé: for them all, it is a question of authorizing, finally, against the nihilist restriction that is the cult of finitude, and even beyond any God, that the infinite *is*.

RB & CG: In his ambitious and provocative reading of *Un coup de dés*, Quentin Meillassoux argues that Mallarmé succeeds in instituting a secular Eucharist. He does so by staging the sacrificial drama of a being—none other than Mallarmé himself—who has become eternal by being identified, through the composition and reception of the poem, with an atheistic infinity, that of infinite chance. Meillassoux therefore closely links the *Coup de dés* to a specific conception of contingency, necessity, and infinity. In your own reading of *Un coup de dés*, but also of a key passage from *Igitur*—"The infinite emerges from chance, which you have denied"—you too propose a specific articulation of these three concepts. For instance, you argue that the event in *Un coup de dés* is absolutely contingent, and that its contingency is negated in the infinite course of a truth procedure. What is at stake for you in Meillassoux's arguments in *The Number and the Siren*? Do you see his understanding of contingency, necessity, and infinity in Mallarmé as consistent with, or opposed to, your own?

AB: On this point, I do not believe that there is a direct opposition between Meillassoux's proposition and my own, as long as it is only a matter of the dialectic between contingency (of the event), necessity (of the laws of the situation), and infinity (of a truth)—even if Meillassoux's references are not, as is normal, entirely my own. I hold that Meillassoux is a very great philosopher, at once passionate and extraordinarily rigorous. The problem between him and myself is very precisely localized: it is the problem posed in your next question!

RB & CG: In his only explicit critique of your reading of *Un coup de dés*, Meillassoux challenges the idea that the poem enjoins us to, as you put it, "[d]ecide from the standpoint of the undecidable" (BE 198), and thereby participate in a truth procedure. By contrast, Meillassoux reads the *PERHAPS* that qualifies the upsurge of the constellation on the eleventh double-page of *Un coup de dés* in starkly minimalist terms. He writes, "the *PERHAPS* is neither realized nor invalidated—it is on the contrary hypostasized, celebrated for itself, erupting in the Heavens as an intrinsic property of the constellation" (EP 38). What is your understanding of the way Meillassoux reads the term *PERHAPS*, specifically as it has implications for a crucial moment in your philosophical system?

AB: With respect to the upsurge of an event, its becoming-truth cannot be declared necessary. In fact, the event opens onto the "perhaps [*peut-être*]" of a truth, and not onto its being. The *peut* of the *peut-être* in fact signifies: "contains the possibility of." Of what? Of the existence of a truth. You must wager that such will be the case and thus decide, at the point of the undecidable, that you will choose to become a faithful subject of the event, and to incorporate yourself into a procedure of truth, regardless of the risks of failure. In this sense, in my view, the "perhaps" does not have to be celebrated, nor, moreover, does it need to be challenged. It is in the nature of the event to only create the possibility, and not the real, of a truth, which depends upon the consequences and thus upon the subjective work that accepts the labour and the trajectory. It is no doubt at this very precise point that I diverge from Meillassoux. He is engaged, whereas I am not, in the direction of a cosmology of contingency, and he tends towards a celebration of the principle of this contingency for very strong reasons: this radical contingency effectively implies it is reasonable to think that every human subject—whoever they are, and even if this means reliving their life—will be saved. For me, sadly, I am unable to follow him. For me, on the one hand, the world as such is necessary, and on the other, truths are contingent on their point of origin, but "will have been" necessary in their infinite becoming. Of course, this is again a matter of a disagreement around religion—just like with Marchal, yet at quite a different level. For Meillassoux, a God of the "perhaps" exists, a weak and infinitely good God, whose whole being, like that of every true goodness, exists only in the perilous trembling of inexistence. This is a very beautiful fiction, but one I am unable to share.

RB & CG: Since the opening to *Logics of Worlds*, you have referred to Mallarmé on fewer and fewer occasions, even if his writings remain a crucial backdrop to your thought. To conclude, could you reflect on the role Mallarmé continues to play in your philosophy? With the forthcoming publication of the final volume of your *Being and Event* trilogy, *The Immanence of Truths*, can you tell us how the poet figures in this work, even at the moments where he is not explicitly invoked?

AB: Everything that I have said in this interview holds. Mallarmé is a definitive source for my thought. I will no doubt make reference to him in *The Immanence of Truths*, in the context of questions concerning the relation between Absoluteness, Finitude, and the plurality of Infinities. I maintain that in a sense, in the space of poetic concentration, Mallarmé said it all.

NOTE

1. Czeslaw Milosz, *The Witness to Poetry* (Cambridge: Harvard University Press), 31.

Biographies

Robert Boncardo has completed a doctorate in French Studies at The University of Sydney and Aix-Marseille Université.

Christian R. Gelder has completed a Master of Arts in English Literature at The Centre for Modernism Studies in Australia, The University of New South Wales.

Further Reading

PRIMARY REFERENCES

Alain Badiou

Badiou, Alain. "Autour de *La parole muette* de Jacques Rancière." *Horlieu*, Vol. 10 No. 18 (2000): 88–95.

Badiou, Alain. *Being and Event*. Translated by Oliver Feltham. London/New York: Continuum, 2005.

Badiou, Alain. *Handbook of Inaesthetics*. Translated by Alberto Toscano. Stanford: Stanford University Press, 2005.

Badiou, Alain. *Briefings on Existence*. Translated by Norman Madarasz. New York: State University of New York Press, 2006.

Badiou, Alain. *Conditions*. Translated by Steven Corcoran. London/New York: Continuum, 2008.

Badiou, Alain. *Number and Numbers*. Translated by Robin Mackay. Cambridge/Malden: Polity Press, 2008.

Badiou, Alain. *Theory of the Subject*. Translated by Bruno Bosteels. London/New York: Continuum, 2009.

Badiou, Alain. *Five Lessons on Wagner*. Translated by Susan Spitzer. London: Verso, 2010.

Badiou, Alain. "Mark and Lack." In *Concept and Form: Volume 1, Key Texts from the Cahiers pour l'Analyse*. Edited by Peter Hallward and Knox Peden. Translated by Zachary Luke Fraser with Ray Brassier, 159–185. London: Verso, 2012.

Badiou, Alain. *Rhapsody for the Theatre*. Translated by Bruno Bosteels. London: Verso, 2013.

Badiou, Alain. "Is it Exact that All Thought Emits A Throw of Dice?" Translated by Robert Boncardo and Christian R. Gelder. *Hyperion*, Vol. 9 No. 3 (2014): 64–86.

Badiou, Alain. *The Age of the Poets: And Other Writings on Twentieth-Century Poetry and Prose*. Translated by Emily Apter and Bruno Bosteels. London: Verso, 2014.

Badiou, Alain and Jean-Claude Milner. *Controversies: A Dialogue on the Politics and Philosophy of our Time*. Translated by Susan Spitzer. Cambridge/Malden: Polity Press, 2014.

Lacoue-Labarthe, Philippe, Jacques Rancière, Jean-François Lyotard, and Alain Badiou. "Liminaire sur l'ouvrage d'Alain Badiou 'L'Être et l'événement.'" *Le Cahier (Collège international de philosophie)* No. 8 (1989): 201–268.

Stéphane Mallarmé

Mallarmé, Stéphane. *Le "Livre" de Mallarmé*. Edited by Jacques Scherer. Paris: Gallimard, 1957.

Mallarmé, Stéphane. *Selected Poetry and Prose*. Translated by Mary Ann Craws. New York, NY: New Directions, 1982.

Mallarmé, Stéphane. *Selected Letters of Stéphane Mallarmé*. Translated by Rosemary Lloyd. Chicago, IL: The University of Chicago Press, 1988.

Mallarmé, Stéphane. *Correspondance: Lettres sur la poésie*. Edited by Bertrand Marchal. Paris: Gallimard, 1995.

Mallarmé, Stéphane. *Collected Poems: A Bilingual Edition*. Translated by Henry Weinfield. Berkeley/Los Angeles/London: University of California Press, 1996.

Mallarmé, Stéphane. *Œuvres complètes I, Édition présentée, établie et annotée par Bertrand Marchal*. Paris: Gallimard, 1998.

Mallarmé, Stéphane. *Œuvres complètes II, Édition présentée, établie et annotée par Bertrand Marchal*. Paris: Gallimard, 2003.

Mallarmé, Stéphane. *Mallarmé in Prose*. Translated by Mary Ann Caws. New York: New Directions, 2001.

Mallarmé, Stéphane. *Igitur, Divagations, Un Coup de dés: Nouvelle édition présentée, établie et annotée par Bertrand Marchal*. Edited by Bertrand Marchal. Paris: Gallimard, 2003.

Mallarmé, Stéphane. *Divagations*. Translated by Barbara Johnson. Cambridge/Massachusetts/London: The Belknap Press of Harvard University Press, 2007.

Mallarmé, Stéphane. *Stéphane Mallarmé: The Poems in Verse*. Translated by Peter Manson. Miami: Miami University Press, 2012.

Jean-Claude Milner

Milner, Jean-Claude. *Ordres et raisons de langue*. Paris: Seuil, 1982.

Milner, Jean-Claude. *Les Noms indistincts*. Paris: Seuil, 1983.

Milner, Jean-Claude. *Introduction à une science du langage*. Paris: Editions du Seuil, 1989.
Milner, Jean-Claude. *For the Love of Language*. Translated by Ann Banfield. London: The Macmillian Press, 1990.
Milner, Jean-Claude. *L'Œuvre claire: Lacan, la science, la philosophie*. Paris: Seuil, 1995.
Milner, Jean-Claude. *Mallarmé au tombeau*. Paris: Verdier, 1999.
Milner, Jean-Claude. "The Doctrine of Science." Translated by Oliver Feltham *Umbr(a): A Journal of the Unconscious: Science and Truth*. (2000): 33–66.
Milner, Jean-Claude. *Constats*. Paris: Folio, 2002.
Milner, Jean-Claude. *Existe-t-il une vie intellectuelle en France?* Paris: Verdier, 2002.
Milner, Jean-Claude. *Les Penchants criminels de l'Europe démocratique*. Paris: Verdier, 2003.
Milner, Jean-Claude. *L'arrogance du présent*. Paris: Grasset, 2009.
Milner, Jean-Claude. "The Traps of the All." Translated by Ed Pluth. *S: Journal for the Circle of Lacanian Ideology Critique*, Vol. 3 (2010): 22–39.
Milner, Jean-Claude. "The Revolution, Infinite Conjunction." Translated by Tzuchien Tho. *S: Journal for the Circle of Lacanian Ideology Critique*, Vol. 3 (2010): 64–69.
Milner, Jean-Claude. "Prose Redeemed." Translated by John Cleary. *S: Journal for the Circle of Lacanian Ideology Critique*, Vol. 3 (2010): 106–113.
Milner, Jean-Claude. "Truth and Exactitude." Translated by Robin M. Muller. *Graduate Faculty Philosophy Journal*, Vol. 31 No. 1 (2010): 25–33.
Milner, Jean-Claude. "The Point of the Signifier." In *Concept and Form, Volume 1: Selections from the Cahiers pour l'analyse*. Edited by Peter Hallward and Knox Peden. Translated by Christian Kerslake. Revised by Knox Peden, 107–118. London: Verso, 2012.
Milner, Jean-Claude. "'The Force of Minimalism': An interview with Jean-Claude Milner." In *Concept and Form, Volume 2: Interviews and essays on Cahiers pour l'Analyse*, 229–244. Edited by Hallward and Peden. London: Verso, 2012.
Milner, Jean-Claude. *Harry Potter: À l'école des sciences morales et politiques*. Paris: PUF, 2014.
Milner, Jean-Claude. "Jean-Claude Milner: Remarks on the name Jew and the universal." Translated by Robert S Kawashima. *Postmedieval*, Vol. 5 No. 3 (2014): 320–335.
Milner, Jean-Claude. "Mallarmé Perchance." Translated by Liesl Yamaguchi. *Hyperion*, Vol. 9, No. 3 (2014): 87–109.
Milner, Jean-Claude. *L'Universel en éclats: Court traité politique 3*. Paris: Verdier, 2014.

Milner, Jean-Claude. "The Tell-Tale Constellations." Translated by Christian R. Gelder. *S: Journal for the Circle of Lacanian Ideology Critique*, Vol. 9 (2016), 'Mallarmé Today'. 31–38.
Milner, Jean-Claude and François Regnault. *Dire le vers*. Paris: Verdier, 1987.

Jacques Rancière

Rancière, Jacques. "La rime et le conflit. La politique du poème." In *Mallarmé ou l'obscurité lumineuse*. Edited by B. Marchal and J. L. Steinmetz. Paris: Hermann, 1998.
Rancière, Jacques. *The Politics of Aesthetics: The Distribution of the Sensible*. Translated by Gabriel Rockhill. London: Continuum, 2006.
Rancière, Jacques. *Aesthetics and its Discontents*. Translated by Steven Corcoran. London: Verso, 2009.
Rancière, Jacques. *The Aesthetic Unconscious*. Translated by Debra Keates and James Swenson. Cambridge: Polity Press, 2009.
Rancière, Jacques. *The Future of the Image*. Translated by Gregory Elliot. London: Verso, 2009.
Rancière, Jacques. *Dissensus: On Politics and Aesthetics*. Edited and translated by Steven Corcoran. London: Continuum, 2010.
Rancière, Jacques. *Mallarmé: The Politics of the Siren*. Translated by Steven Corcoran. New York, NY: Continuum, 2011.
Rancière, Jacques. *Mute Speech*. Translated by Gabriel Rockhill. New York, NY: Columbia University Press, 2011.
Rancière, Jacques. *The Politics of Literature*. Translated by Julie Rose. Cambridge: Polity Press. 2011.
Rancière, Jacques. *Aisthesis: Scenes from the Aesthetic Regime of Art*. Translated by Zakir Paul. London, NY: Verso, 2013.

SECONDARY REFERENCES

Benoit, Eric. *Mallarmé et le mystère du "Livre."* Paris: Honoré Champion, 1998.
Benoit, Eric. *Néant Sonore: Mallarmé ou la traversée des paradoxes*. Genève: Droz, 2007.
Blanchot, Maurice. *Faux Pas*. Translated by Charlotte Mandel. Stanford, CA: Stanford University Press, 2001.
Blanchot, Maurice. *The Book to Come*. Translated by Charlotte Mandel. Stanford, CA: Stanford University Press, 2003.
Blay, Michel. *Reasoning with the Infinite: From the Closed World to the Mathematical Universe*. Translated by M. B. DeBevoise. Chicago, IL: The University of Chicago Press 1998.

Boncardo, Robert. "Mallarmé in Alain Badiou's *Theory of the Subject.*" *Hyperion*, Vol. 9, No. 3 (2014): 1–45.
Boutroux, Émile. *The Contingency of the Laws of Nature*. Translated by Fred Rothwell. Chicago: The Open Court Publishing Company, 1920.
Campion, Pierre. *Mallarmé, poésie et philosophie*. Paris: PUF, 1994.
Cassedy, Steven. "Mathematics, Relationalism, and the Rise of Modern Literary Aesthetics." *Journal of the History of Ideas* Vol. 49, No. 1 (1988): 109–132.
Cassedy, Steven. "Mallarmé and Andrej Belyj: Mathematics and the Phenomenality of the Literary Object." *MLN* Vol. 96, No. 5 (1981): 1066–1083.
Cassedy, Steven. *Flight from Eden: The Origins of Modern Literary Criticism and Theory*. Berkeley: University of California Press, 1990.
Cohn, Robert Greer. *Towards the Poems of Mallarmé*. Berkley: University of California Press, 1965.
Davies, Gardner. *Vers une explication rationnelle du 'Coup de Dés'*. Paris: Librairie José Corti, 1953.
Davies, Gardner. *Mallarmé et le Drame Solaire*. Paris: Librairie José Corti, 1959.
Davies, Gardner. *Mallarmé et la couche suffisante d'intelligibilité*. Paris: Librairie José Corti, 1988.
Deleuze, Gilles. *Nietzsche and Philosophy*. Translated by Hugh Tomlinson. New York: Columbia University Press, 1983.
Deleuze, Gilles. *The Fold: Leibniz and the Baroque*. Translated by Tom Conley. London: Continuum, 1993.
Derrida, Jacques. "The Double Session." In *Dissemination*. Translated by Barbara Johnson, 173–286. Chicago, IL: The University of Chicago Press, 1981.
Durand, Pascal. *Mallarmé: Du sens des formes au sens des formalités*. Paris: Editions du Seuil, 2008.
Eyers, Tom. *Post-Rationalism: Psychoanalysis, Epistemology, and Marxism in Post-War France*. London: Bloomsbury, 2013.
Foucault, Michel. *The Order of Things: An Archaeology of the Human Sciences*. New York, NY: Vintage Books, 1994.
Gibson, Andrew. *Beckett and Badiou: The Pathos of Intermittency*. Oxford: Oxford University Press, 2006.
Gelder, Christian R. "The Murmur of Nothing: Mallarmé and Mathematics." In *Aesthetics after Finitude: An Anthology of Essays*. Edited by Baylee Brits, Pure Gibson and Amy Ireland. Melbourne: Re.Press, 2016: 157–169.
Hamel, Jean-François. *Camarade Mallarmé: Une Politique de la lecture*. Paris: Editions de Minuit, 2014.
Hyppolite, Jean. "Le Coup de dés de Stéphane Mallarmé et le message." *Les Études philosophiques*, No. 4 (1958): 463–468.
Jacquod, Valérie. *Le roman symboliste: un art de l'extrême conscience: Edouard Dujardin, André Gide, Rémy de Gourmont, Marcel Schwob*. Paris: Droz, 2008.

James, Alison. "Poetic Form and the Crisis of Community: Revisiting Rancière's Aesthetics." In Joseph Acquisto, *Thinking Poetry: Philosophical Approaches to Nineteenth-Century French Poetry*. 167–183. London: Palgrave MacMillan, 2013.

Kaufmann, Vincent. *La faute à Mallarmé: l'aventure de la théorie littéraire*. Paris: Editons du Seuil, 2011.

Koyré, Alexandre. *From the Closed World to the Infinite Universe*. Baltimore, MD: The Johns Hopkins Press, 1957.

Kristeva, Julia. *Sèméiôtiké: Recherches pour une sémanalyse*. Paris: Editions du Seuil, 1969.

Kristeva, Julia. *La révolution du langage poétique: L'avant-garde à la fin du XIXème siècle: Lautréamont et Mallarmé*. Paris: Editions du Seuil, 1974.

Kristeva, Julia. "Towards a Semiology of Paragrams." In *The Tel Quel Reader*, edited by Patrick ffrench and Roland-François Lack. Translated by Roland-François Lack, 25–49. New York, NY: Routledge, 1998.

Lloyd, Rosemary. *Mallarmé, The Poet and his Circle*. New York, NY: Cornell University Press, 1999.

Lyotard, Jean-François. *Discourse, Figure*. Translated by Anthony Hudek and Mary Lydon. Minneapolis, Minnesota: University of Minnesota Press, 2011.

Marchal, Bertrand. *Lecture de Mallarmé: Poésies, Igitur, le Coup de dés*. Paris: Librairie José Corti, 1985.

Marchal, Bertrand. *La Religion de Mallarmé: poésie, mythologie et religion*. Paris: Librairie José Corti, 1988.

Meillassoux, Quentin. *The Number and the Siren: A Decipherment of Mallarmé's Un Coup de dés*. Translated by Robin Mackay. New York, NY: Urbanomic/Sequence, 2012.

Meillassoux, Quentin. "Badiou and Mallarmé: The Event and the Perhaps." Translated by Alyosha Edlebi. *Parrhesia*, No. 16 (2013): 35–47.

Meillassoux, Quentin. "The *Coup de dés*, or the Materialist Divinization of the Hypothesis." *Collapse*, Vol. 8 (2014): 813–846.

Meillassoux, Quentin. "The Coup de dés, Encoded Crypt." Translated by Robert Boncardo and Christian R. Gelder. *Hyperion*, forthcoming January 2017.

Miller, Jacques-Alain. "Suture (Elements of the Logic of the Signifier)." In *Concept and Form: Volume 1, Key Texts from the Cahiers pour l'Analyse*, edited by Peter Hallward and Knox Peden. Translated by Jacqueline Rose, 91–101. London: Verso, 2012.

Noulet, Emilie. *L'Œuvre poétique de Stéphane Mallarmé*. Paris: Droz, 1940.

Œhler, Dolf. *Le Spleen contre l'oubli: Juin 1848. Baudelaire, Flaubert, Heine, Herzen*. Paris: Payot, 1988.

Richard, Jean-Pierre. *L'Univers imaginaire de Mallarmé*. Paris: Editions du Seuil, 1961.

Roger, Thierry. *L'Archive du Coup de dés*. Paris: Éditions Classiques Garnier, 2010.
Roger, Thierry. "Camarade Mallarmé': mallarmisme, anachronisme, présentisme." *Acta fabula*, "Réinvestissement, rumeur & récriture," Vol. 15, No. 6 (2014).
Roger, Thierry. "Art and Anarchy in the Time of Symbolism: Mallarmé and his Literary Group." Translated by Robert Boncardo. *S: Journal of the Circle for Lacanian Ideology Critique*, 'Mallarmé Today': Forthcoming.
Sartre, Jean-Paul. *Mallarmé, or the Poet of Nothingness*. Translated by Ernest Sturm. Pennsylvania, MD: Pennsylvania State University Press, 1988.
Sartre, Jean-Paul. *The Family Idiot. Gustave Flaubert 1821–1857. Volume 5*. Chicago, IL: The University of Chicago Press, 1993.
Stanguennec, André. *Mallarmé et l'éthique de la poésie*. Paris: Vrin, 1992.
Thibaudet, Albert. *La poésie de Stéphane Mallarmé*. Paris: Gallimard, 2006
Tho, Tzuchien. "The Void Just Ain't (What it Used to Be): Void, Infinity, and the Indeterminate." *Filozofski vestnik* Vol. 34, No. 2 (2013): 27–48.
Valéry, Paul. *Leonardo, Poe, Mallarmé*. Translated by Malcolm Cowley and James R. Lawler. London: Routledge, 1972.
Williams, Heather. *Mallarmé's Ideas in Language*. Bern: Peter Lang, 2004.

Index

Alain Badiou; *Being and Event*, 14, 15, 18–19, 20–21, 25, 54, 87–88; *Conditions*, 19–20, 24, 54; *Five Lessons on Wagner*, 91; *Handbook of Inaesthetics*, 89; 'Is it Exact that All Thought Emits a Throw of Dice?", 25; *Logics of Worlds*, 91, 95; *Manifesto for Philosophy*, 19, 87; "Mark and Lack", 15, 16–18, 84; *Of an Obscure Disaster*, 76; *Short Treatise on Transitory Ontology*, 22, 93; "The Current Situation on the Philosophical Front", 86; *The Immanence of Truths*, 95–96; *Theory of the Subject*, 23, 54, 84, 85–87, 90
Adorno, Theodor, 54
Althusser, Louis, 17, 55
Aragon, Louis, 29

Barthes, Roland, 59
Baudelaire, Charles, 26, 27, 60, 64, 66, 67; "Le Cygne", 26, 67
Blanchot, Maurice, 3, 41, 83, 84
Boulez, Pierre, 83

Boutroux, Émile, 13
Brecht, Bertolt, 29
Blair, Tony, 73

Cantor, Georg, 18, 22, 93
Pierre Campion, 3
Cahiers pour l'analyse, 15–16, 59, 84
Chalamov, Varlam, 79–80
Change, 22, 83
Chassé, Charles, 43
Cicero, Marcus Tullius, 72
Claudel, Paul, 71, 81

Davies, Gardner, 21, 38, 84, 90
de Banville, Théodore, 52
de Gaulle, Charles, 71
Derrida, Jacques, 3, 41, 60, 88; "The Double Session", 51–53, 59
Deleuze, Gilles, 3
Diana, Princess of Wales, 73
Diderot, Denis, 46

Faye, Jean-Pierre, 38, 39 n. 49, 42, 83

Flaubert, Gustave, 42, 75;
  Bouvard and Pécuchet, 57;
  Salammbô, 77, 80
Foucault, Michel, 3, 59, 60
Frege, Gottlob, 16
Freud, Sigmund, 61

Galileo Galilei, 6, 11, 22, 61, 62,
  63, 93, 94
Gautier, Théophile, 52
Gide, André, 69, 70
Gödel, Kurt, 63

Hamel, Jean-François, 34
Hegel, G. W. F, 23, 32, 90
Heidegger, Martin, 54
Hölderlin, Friedrich, 5, 51
Hugo, Victor, 5, 15, 26, 27, 51, 61,
  64, 65, 66, 67, 69, 71, 75, 89; *La
  légende des siècles*, 26
Hyppolite, Jean, 3

Jakobson, Roman, 60, 80
James, Alison, 4
Jacquod, Valérie, 39
Johnson, Barbara, 2
Joyce, James; *Finnegans Wake*, 57

Kahn, Gustave, 44
Koyré, Alexandre, 11
Kristeva, Julia, 2, 3, 4; "Poetry and
  Negativity", 6; *Revolution in
  Poetic Language*, 6
Lacan, Jacques, 6, 9, 10, 12, 23,
  60, 77, 85; *lalangue*, 4, 7–8;
  "Logical Time and the Assertion
  of Anticipated Certainty: A New
  Sophism", 77; *L'Etourdit*, 7;
  Seminar XX 7
Lacoue-Labarthe, Philippe, 14, 91
Laforgue, Jules, 44
Lautréamont, Comte de, 84

Lenin, Vladimir, 67, 69, 77
Lévi-Strauss, Claude, 40
Lyotard, Jean-François 3, 20

Malevitch, Kazimir, 43
Mallarmé, Stéphane; "À la nue
  accablante tu", 19, 24, 24, 91;
  "An Interrupted Spectacle",
  30–31; "Conflict", 47, 48;
  "Confrontation", 48; "Crisis of
  Verse", 3, 8, 9; *Igitur*, 3, 85, 94;
  "L'Après-midi d'un faune", 20;
  "Las de l'amer repos", 29–30;
  "Le vierge, le vivace et le bel
  aujourd'hui", 25–28, 29, 64, 66,
  68, 92; *Les Mots anglais*, 1, 74;
  "Music and Letters", 13; *Notes
  sur le langage*, 3, 14, 74; *Pour un
  tombeau d'Anatole*, 79, 80; 'Prose
  (pour des Esseintes)', 20, 62;
  "Solemnity", 5; Sonnet
  en -yx, 19–20, 85, 91; The Book,
  11, 13, 28, 45, 54, 60, 64, 66, 67,
  68–69, 70; "The Book, Spiritual
  Instrument", 3; "The Demon of
  Analogy", 28, 66; *Un Coup de
  dés*, 3, 7, 7, 9–11, 13, 15,
  20–21, 28, 32–34, 40, 45–46, 56,
  63, 64, 65, 66, 67, 68, 78–79, 84,
  85, 86, 88, 91, 93, 94
Mao Tse-tung, 86
Marchal, Bertrand, 78, 92, 95; *La
  Religion de Mallarmé*, 5, 50–51,
  90–91
Marguerite, Paul, 52
Meillassoux, Quentin, 78, 88, 91;
  The Number and the Siren, 56, 64,
  94–95; "Badiou and Mallarmé:
  The Event and the Perhaps",
  94–95
Meillet, Antoine, 61
Michel, Natacha, 65

Miller, Jacques-Alain, 85; "Suture (Elements of the Logic of the Signifier)", 16, 17, 84
Milner, Jean-Claude; *Constats*, 73, 76–78, 92; "Existe-t-il une vie intellectuelle française ?", 20; *For the Love of Language*, 7–9; *Introduction à une science du langage*, 10; *Les noms indistincts*, 9, 13, 40; *Les penchants criminels de l'Europe démocratique*, 79; *L'Œuvre claire*, 11; *L'Universel en éclats*, 78; "Mallarmé Perchance", 9, 11, 28; *Mallarmé au tombeau*, 4, 25–29, 55–56, 64, 66, 67, 69, 72, 74, 76, 78, 80, 92; "The Tell-Tale Constellations", 13–14, 62, 63, 66, 67, 93
Milosz, Czeslaw; *The Witness of Poetry*, 89
Musil, Robert; *The Man Without Qualities*, 57

Nancy, Jean-Luc, 14
Neruda, Pablo, 29
Newton, Isaac, 22, 94
Noverre, Jean-George, 46

Œhler, Dolf, 26

Popper, Karl, 12
Plato, 33, 45, 51–53, 77
Poe, Edgar Allan, 75; *Eureka*, 62
Proust, Marcel, 47, 57, 70
Rancière, Jacques; *Aisthesis*, 43; *Mute Speech*, 5, 31, 35; *On the Shores of Politics*, 43; *Politics of the Siren*, 4–5, 29–35, 42, 53, 56, 74–76, 91–92; *Proletarian Nights*, 43, 48; *The Names of History*, 43
Regnault, François, 65
Richard, Jean-Pierre, 90
Rimbaud, Arthur, 19, 51, 84
Rivière, Jacques, 70
Roger, Thierry, 2, 3
Ronat, Mitsou, 2, 65
Roubaud, Jacques, 65
Rowling, J. K., 73, 74; *Fantastic Beasts and Where to Find Them*, 81; *Harry Potter*, 72
Rilke, Rainer Maria, 57
Russian Formalists, 4

Saint-Simonism, 6, 48, 50
Sartre, Jean-Paul, 3, 22, 41, 43, 49, 59, 83, 84, 92
Saussure, Ferdinand, 9, 10, 61, 80
Scherer, Jacques, 39, 60
Schönberg, Arnold, 43
Sollers Philippe, 38, 83
Stanguennec, André, 3

Tel Quel, 22, 41, 42, 49, 52, 59, 83, 84, 86
Tho, Tzuchien, 16

Valéry, Paul, 22, 41, 69, 70, 90
Verne, Jules, 74
Villiers de l'Isle-Adam, Auguste, 23
Vitez, Antoine, 90

Wagner, Richard, 6, 31–32, 48, 51, 68

www.ingramcontent.com/pod-product-compliance
Lightning Source LLC
Chambersburg PA
CBHW031554300426
44111CB00006BA/307